A Brand New School Story

THE

By the Author of FRINDLE

LANDRY NEWS

ANDREW CLEMENTS

ILLUSTRATIONS BY
BRIAN SELZNICK

This edition is published by special arrangement with Simon & Schuster
Books for Young Readers, an Imprint of Simon & Schuster Children's
Publishing Division and Brian Selznick.

For permission to reprint copyrighted material, grateful acknowledgment
is made to the following sources:

Brian Selznick: Illustrations by Brian Selznick from *The Landry News* by
Andrew Clements. Illustrations copyright © 2000 by Brian Selznick.

*Simon & Schuster Books For Young Readers, an Imprint of Simon &
Schuster Children's Publishing Division: The Landry News* by Andrew
Clements. Text copyright © 1999 by Andrew Clements.

Printed in the United States of America

ISBN 10 0-15-365169-5
ISBN 13 978-0-15-365169-4

1 2 3 4 5 6 7 8 9 10   947 17 16 14 13 12 11 10 09 08 07 06

THE
LANDRY NEWS

For my brother Denney—
a good writer, a good journalist,
a good man

✳✳✳✳✳✳✳✳✳✳✳✳✳✳✳ The Bill

Congress of the United States
begun and held at the City of New-York, on Wednesday the
fourth of March, one thousand seven hundred and eighty nine.

✳

The Conventions of a number of the States, having at the time of their adopting the Constitution, expressed a desire, in order to prevent misconstruction or abuse of its powers, that further declaratory and restrictive clauses should be added: And as extending the ground of public confidence in the Government, will best ensure the beneficent ends of its institution.

Resolved by the Senate and House of Representatives of the United States of America, in Congress assembled, two thirds of both Houses concurring, that the following Articles be proposed to the Legislatures of the several States as amendments to the Constitution of the United States, all, or any of which articles, when ratified by three fourths of the said Legislatures, to be valid to all intents and purposes, as part of the said Constitution; viz.

Articles in addition to, and Amendment of the Constitution of the United States of America, proposed by Congress and ratified by the Legislatures of the several States, pursuant to the fifth Article of the original Constitution.

✳✳✳

Amendment I
Congress shall make no law respecting an establishment of religion, or prohibiting the free exercise thereof; or abridging the freedom of speech, or of the press; or the right of the people peaceably to assemble, and to petition the Government for a redress of grievances.

Amendment II
A well regulated Militia, being necessary to the security of a free State, the right of the people to keep and bear Arms, shall not be infringed.

Amendment III
No Soldier shall, in time of peace be quartered in any house, without the consent of the Owner, nor in time of war, but in a manner to be prescribed by law.

# of Rights ✳✳✳✳✳✳✳✳✳✳✳✳✳✳✳✳

Amendment IV

The right of the people to be secure in their persons, houses, papers, and effects, against unreasonable searches and seizures, shall not be violated, and no Warrants shall issue, but upon probable cause, supported by Oath or affirmation, and particularly describing the place to be searched, and the persons or things to be seized.

Amendment V

No person shall be held to answer for a capital, or otherwise infamous crime, unless on a presentment or indictment of a Grand Jury, except in cases arising in the land or naval forces, or in the Militia, when in actual service in time of War or public danger; nor shall any person be subject for the same offence to be twice put in jeopardy of life or limb; nor shall be compelled in any criminal case to be a witness against himself, nor be deprived of life, liberty, or property, without due process of law; nor shall private property be taken for public use, without just compensation.

Amendment VI

In all criminal prosecutions, the accused shall enjoy the right to a speedy and public trial, by an impartial jury of the State and district wherein the crime shall have been committed, which district shall have been previously ascertained by law, and to be informed of the nature and cause of the accusation; to be confronted with the witnesses against him; to have compulsory process for obtaining witnesses in his favor, and to have the Assistance of Counsel for his defence.

Amendment VII

In suits at common law, where the value in controversy shall exceed twenty dollars, the right of trial by jury shall be preserved, and no fact tried by a jury, shall be otherwise reexamined in any Court of the United States, than according to the rules of the common law.

Amendment VIII

Excessive bail shall not be required, nor excessive fines imposed, nor cruel and unusual punishments inflicted.

Amendment IX

The enumeration in the Constitution, of certain rights, shall not be construed to deny or disparage others retained by the people.

Amendment X

The powers not delegated to the United States by the Constitution, nor prohibited by it to the States, are reserved to the States respectively, or to the people.

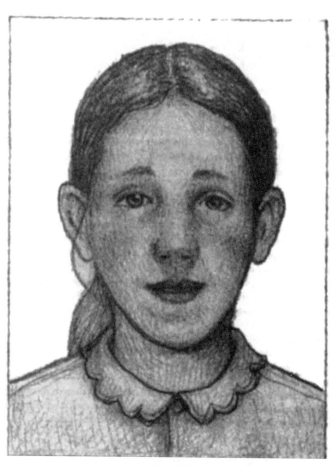

Cara Landry, editor in chief of *The Landry News*, and star of this story.

CHAPTER 1

NEW KID GETS OLD TEACHER

"CARA LOUISE, I am *talking* to you!"

Cara Landry didn't answer her mom. She was busy.

She sat at the gray folding table in the kitchenette, a heap of torn paper scraps in front of her. Using a roll of clear tape, Cara was putting the pieces back together. Little by little, they fell into place on a fresh sheet of paper about eighteen inches wide. The top part was already taking shape—a row of neat block letters, carefully drawn to look like newspaper type.

"Cara, honey, you *promised* you wouldn't start that again. Didn't you learn one little thing from the last time?"

Cara's mom was talking about what had happened at the school Cara had attended for most of fourth grade, just after her dad had left. There had been some problems.

"Don't worry, Mom," Cara said absentmindedly, absorbed in her task.

Cara Landry had only lived in Carlton for six months. From the day she moved to town, during April of fourth grade, everyone had completely ignored her. She had been easy for the other kids to ignore. Just another brainy, quiet girl, the kind who always turns in assignments on time, always aces tests. She dressed in a brown plaid skirt and a clean white blouse every day, dependable as the tile pattern on the classroom floor. Average height, skinny arms and legs, white socks, black shoes. Her light brown hair was always pulled back into a thin ponytail, and her pale blue eyes hardly ever connected with anyone else's. As far as the other kids were concerned, Cara was there, but just barely.

All that changed in one afternoon soon after Cara started fifth grade.

It was like any other Friday for Cara at Denton Elementary School. Math first thing in the morning, then science and gym, lunch and health, and finally, reading, language arts, and social studies in Mr. Larson's room.

Mr. Larson was the kind of teacher parents write letters to the principal about, letters like:

Dear Dr. Barnes:
   We know our child is only in second grade this

year, but please be *sure* that he [or she] is NOT put into Mr. Larson's class for fifth grade.

Our lawyer tells us that we have the right to make our educational choices known to the principal and that you are not allowed to tell anyone we have written you this letter.

So in closing, we again urge you to take steps to see that our son [or daughter] is *not* put into Mr. Larson's classroom.

Sincerely yours,

Mr. and Mrs. Everybody-who-lives-in-Carlton

Still, *someone* had to be in Mr. Larson's class; and if your mom was always too tired to join the PTA or a volunteer group, and if you mostly hung out at the library by yourself or sat around your apartment reading and doing homework, it was possible to live in Carlton for half a year and not know that Mr. Larson was a lousy teacher. And if your mom didn't know enough to write a letter to the principal, you were pretty much guaranteed to get Mr. Larson.

Mr. Larson said he believed in the open classroom. At parents' night every September, Mr. Larson explained that children learn best when they learn things on their own.

This was not a new idea. This idea about learning was being used successfully by practically every teacher in America.

But Mr. Larson used it in his own special way. Almost every day, he would get the class started on a story or a worksheet or a word list or some reading and then go to his desk, pour some coffee from his big red thermos, open up his newspaper, and sit.

Over the years, Mr. Larson had taught himself how to ignore the chaos that erupted in his classroom every day. Unless there was the sound of breaking glass, screams, or splintering furniture, Mr. Larson didn't even look up. If other teachers or the principal complained about the noise, he would ask a student to shut the door, and then go back to reading his newspaper.

Even though Mr. Larson had not done much day-to-day teaching for a number of years, quite a bit of learning happened in room 145 anyway. The room itself had a lot to do with that. Room 145 was like a giant educational glacier, with layer upon layer of accumulated materials. Mr. Larson read constantly, and every magazine he had subscribed to or purchased during the past twenty years had ended up in his classroom. *Time, Good Housekeeping, U.S. News & World Report, Smithsonian, Cricket, Rolling Stone, National Geographic, Boys' Life, Organic Gardening, The New Yorker, Life, Highlights, Fine Woodworking, Reader's Digest, Popular Mechanics*, and dozens of others. Heaps of them filled the shelves and cluttered the corners. Newspapers, too, were stacked in front of the windows;

recent ones were piled next to Mr. Larson's chair. This stack was almost level with his desktop, and it made a convenient place to rest his coffee cup.

Each square inch of wall space and a good portion of the ceiling were covered with maps, old report covers, newspaper clippings, diagrammed sentences, cartoons, Halloween decorations, a cursive handwriting chart, quotations from the Gettysburg Address and the Declaration of Independence, and the complete Bill of Rights—a dizzying assortment of historical, grammatical, and literary information.

The bulletin boards were like huge paper time warps—shaggy, colorful collages. Whenever Mr. Larson happened to find an article or a poster or an illustration that looked interesting, he would staple it up, and he always invited the kids to do the same. But for the past eight or ten years, Mr. Larson had not bothered to take down the old papers—he just wallpapered over them with the new ones. Every few months—especially when it was hot and humid—the weight of the built-up paper would become too much for the staples, and a slow avalanche of clippings would lean forward and whisper to the floor. When that happened, a student repair committee would grab some staplers from the supply cabinet, and the room would shake as they pounded flat pieces of history back onto the wall.

Freestanding racks of books were scattered all

around room 145. There were racks loaded with mysteries, Newbery winners, historical fiction, biographies, and short stories. There were racks of almanacs, nature books, world records books, old encyclopedias, and dictionaries. There was even a rack of well-worn picture books for those days when fifth-graders felt like looking back at the books they grew up on.

The reading corner was jammed with pillows and was sheltered by half of an old cardboard geodesic dome. The dome had won first prize at a school fair about fifteen years ago. Each triangle of the dome had been painted blue or yellow or green and was designed by kids to teach something—like the flags of African nations or the presidents of the United States or the last ten Indianapolis-500 winners—dozens and dozens of different minilessons. The dome was missing half its top and looked a little like an igloo after a week of warm weather. Still, every class period there would be a scramble to see which small group of friends would take possession of the dome.

The principal didn't approve of Mr. Larson's room one bit. It gave him the creeps. Dr. Barnes liked things to be spotless and orderly, like his own office—a place for everything, and everything in its place. Occasionally he threatened to make Mr. Larson change rooms—but there was really no other room he could move to. Besides, room 145 was on the lower level of the school in the back corner. It was the room that was the farthest away from the office, and Dr. Barnes couldn't bear the thought of Mr. Larson being one inch closer to him.

Even though it was chaotic and cluttered, Mr. Larson's class suited Cara Landry just fine. She was able to tune out the noise, and she liked being left alone for the last two hours of every day. She would always get to class early and pull a desk and chair over to the back corner by some low bookcases. Then she would pull the large map tripod up behind her chair. She would spread out her books and papers on the bookshelf to her right, and she would tack her plastic pencil case on the bulletin board to her left. It was a small private space, like her own little office, where Cara could just sit and read, think, and write.

Then, on the first Friday afternoon in October, Cara took what she'd been working on and without saying anything to anybody, she used four thumbtacks and stuck it onto the overloaded bulletin board at the back of Mr. Larson's room. It was Denton Elementary School's first edition of *The Landry News*.

CHAPTER 2

ROOF BLOWS OFF SCHOOLROOM

AFTER THE COMICS and the crossword puzzle, the sports section was Mr. Larson's favorite part of the newspaper. He always saved the sports for the last hour of the day, as a reward for himself. On this particular Friday afternoon in October, Mr. Larson was reading an important article about the baseball pennant races. He was trying hard to give the article his full attention, but he couldn't.

Something was wrong.

There were no shattering windows, no toppling chairs, no screaming or yelling. It was worse than that. It was too quiet.

Mr. Larson looked up from his paper and saw all twenty-three kids gathered around the bulletin board. Some girls were giggling, there were some gasps and pokes and whispers, and some of the bigger boys were elbowing to get in closer. Over the top of his reading glasses, the scene came into focus for Mr. Larson, and he could see what they were staring at: a large sheet of paper laid out in columns, with a banner at the top, *The Landry News*.

Mr. Larson smiled. It was a pleased, self-satisfied smile. "There—you see," he said to himself, as if he were talking to the principal, "*that* is my open classroom at work! Here's living proof. I have not been involved one bit, and that quiet new girl—Laura . . . or Tara? Or . . . well . . . that little Landry girl—she has gone right ahead and made her own newspaper! And look! Just look! All the other kids are getting involved in the learning!" Mr. Larson kept talking to himself, now imagining that he was defending himself in front of the whole school board. "Go right ahead. You're the principal, Dr. Barnes. You can put all the letters you want into my file, Dr. Barnes. But here's proof, right here! I *do* know what I'm doing, and *I'm* the teacher in my classroom, not you!"

Mr. Larson carefully folded up his newspaper and put it onto the large stack beside his desk. He would have to finish that World Series article on Monday.

He carefully straightened his long legs under his desk, then tensed his back and stretched his arms, tilting his head slowly from side to side. He was getting ready to stand up. This was the perfect time for some meaningful interaction with the class. Also, it was only five minutes before the end of the day, and he'd have to stand up then anyway because he had bus duty this week.

Moving carefully among the jumble of desks and

chairs, Mr. Larson got close enough to the bulletin board to read *The Landry News*. He nodded at the headline of the lead story: SECOND-GRADER GAGS ON OVERCOOKED JELL-O. Mr. Larson remembered. That little problem had required a call to 911.

A sports column caught his eye, and squinting, he could read the neatly printed description of a noon-recess touch football game. The game had ended with a fist fight and one-day suspensions for three fifth-grade boys. Mr. Larson read slowly, smiling in approval. The writing was clear, no spelling mistakes, no wasted words. This girl had talent. He was just about to turn and compliment . . . Sara? . . . no—well, the Landry girl, when something caught his eye.

It was in the editorial section. There, in the lower right-hand corner of the paper, Mr. Larson saw his own name. He started reading.

From the Editor's Desk
A Question of Fairness

There has been no teaching so far this year in Mr. Larson's classroom. There has been learning, but there has been no teaching. There is a teacher in the classroom, but he does not teach.

In his handout from parents' night, Mr. Larson says that in his classroom "the students must learn how to learn by themselves, and they must learn to learn from each other, too."

So here is the question: If the students teach themselves, and they also teach each other, why is Mr. Larson the one who gets paid for being a teacher?

In the public records at the Carlton Memorial Library it shows that Mr. Larson got paid $39,324 last year. If that money was paid to the real teachers in Mr. Larson's classroom, then each student would get $9.50 every day during the whole school year. I don't know about you, but that would definitely help my attitude toward school.

And that's the view this week from the News desk.

Cara Landry, Editor in Chief

The kids watched Mr. Larson's face as he stood there reading. His jaw slowly clenched—tighter and tighter. His face reddened, and his short blond hair seemed to bristle all over his head. Instinctively, the kids backed away, clearing a path between Mr. Larson and the bulletin board. With one long stride he was there, and the four thumbtacks shot off and skittered across the floor as he tore the paper down.

Mr. Larson was tall—six feet, two inches. Now he seemed twice that size to the kids. He turned slowly from left to right, looking down at their faces. Without raising his voice he said, "There is a kind of writing that is appropriate in school, and there is a kind that is INappropriate." Turning back to look directly at Cara, he held up the sheet and shook it. "THIS," he shouted, "is INappropriate!"

Folding the paper in half, he walked quickly to his desk, ripping the sheet into smaller and smaller bits as he went. It was deathly still. Mr. Larson turned to look at Cara, still standing beside the bulletin board. Her face was as pale as his was red, and she was biting her lower lip, but she didn't flinch. No one dared to breathe. The silence was shattered by the bell, and as Mr. Larson dropped the shredded paper into the trash basket, he barked, "Class dismissed!"

The room emptied in record time, and Cara was swept along toward the lockers and the waiting buses. Mr. Larson was right behind, on his way to bus duty. He hurried out to the curb, still angry but back under control. The hubbub and confusion of the scene was a welcome distraction, and during the next ten minutes buses one, two, and three filled up and pulled away with their noisy loads.

The last person to get on to bus 4 was Cara Landry. She was running, dragging her jacket, her gray backpack heavy on her thin shoulders.

Mr. Larson did not smile, but he did manage to say, "Good-bye, Cara." He knew her name now.

As she climbed aboard, he turned quickly and went

Karl Larson, a teacher at Denton Elementary School, holding *The Landry News*. He has called it "INappropriate."

back into the school. Bus 4 pulled away.

Mr. Larson went to the teachers' room, got his empty lunch bag off the shelf, and went straight from there out the back door of the school to the staff parking lot. He did not return to room 145 to get his red thermos of coffee. He did not want to go back there until he had to, until Monday.

And it's a good thing he didn't go get his thermos. Because if he had gone into the room and up to his desk, he probably would have glanced down into the wastebasket. And he would have seen that every scrap of *The Landry News* was gone.

Someone had returned to the empty room to pick up all the pieces.

CHAPTER 3

ANCIENT HISTORY, MODERN MYSTERY

THERE WERE SIXTEEN fifth-graders on Cara's bus, and seven of them had been in Mr. Larson's class. Cara usually sat by herself on the bus, but today LeeAnn Ennis slipped into the seat beside her.

As the bus pulled away LeeAnn looked over her shoulder to watch Mr. Larson stomp back into the school. "He was so mad! I've never even heard of him getting mad before. But he was mad today, real mad. I can't believe you wrote that, Cara! Oh . . . you know, I don't think we ever met, but I'm in Mr. Larson's class with you."

"I know who you are," said Cara. "You're LeeAnn Ennis. Ellen Hatcher is your best friend, you like Deke Deopolis, your sister is a cheerleader at the high school, and your mom is secretary of the Denton School PTA. Math is your favorite subject, you love cats, and you went to the big sleepover party at Betsy

Lowenstein's house last weekend."

LeeAnn's mouth dropped open. "What, are you a spy or something? How do you know all that?"

Feeling embarrassed, Cara smiled, something LeeAnn had never seen her do before. "No, I'm not a spy. I'm a journalist. People who make newspapers need to know what's going on, that's all. When things happen, or when people say things, I just pay attention."

Ed Thomson and Joey DeLucca were in the seat right behind LeeAnn and Cara, and they were listening. They were in Mr. Larson's class, too.

Joey leaned forward over the seat and looked at Cara. "You mean you know stuff like that about *everybody*?"

"No, not everybody. Some people are newsmakers and some aren't." Cara blushed. She thought Joey was cute. He had never said a word to her until now. Somehow, she made herself talk naturally. "It's not like I memorize all this stuff or anything. But if something happens that might be news, then I ask questions and pay attention so I can report on it. News has got to be accurate. Like that kid who choked on the rubber Jell-O? That was Alan Cortez. He's in second grade in Mrs. Atkins's class. The lady in the kitchen who cooked the Jell-O that day is Alice Rentsler. The principal made her write a letter of apology to Alan's parents. Alice also had to have a special Jell-O-making session with the kitchen supervisor to make sure she cooks it right from now on.

I thought that was all pretty interesting, so I looked around and I got the facts."

Ed piped up. "But all that stuff about LeeAnn? What's that about? Is she such a big newsmaker?" LeeAnn narrowed her eyes at Ed and pretended like she was going to whack him with her backpack.

Cara smiled and said, "No, that's just stuff I've noticed—or heard kids talk about. LeeAnn has cat stickers all over her notebook and her locker, her mom's name is on the PTA newsletter we got in the mail at my house this summer, her big sister drops LeeAnn off at school sometimes when she's wearing her cheerleader outfit, and everybody knows that LeeAnn likes Deke."

Ed was impressed. "Okay, okay . . . all that makes sense. But tell me why you wrote that thing about Mr. Larson. Are you mad at him or something?"

Cara didn't answer right away. "No, I'm not mad at him," she said thoughtfully. "I just don't think it's right that he doesn't teach us anything." Cara was quiet while about ten kids got up and pushed and shuffled and yelled their way off the bus. Her stop was next.

As the bus lurched forward again, Cara lowered her voice and said, "Can you guys keep a secret?" Joey and LeeAnn and Ed nodded. "Promise?" All three kids nodded again, leaning closer. Looking from face to face, Cara said, "Have you ever looked in those glass cases in the front hall by the office?"

"You mean all the sports trophies?" asked Joey. "Yeah, I've seen them."

Cara said, "Well, you're right, it's mostly sports, but there's some other stuff there, too—Writer of the Month awards, and Math Club honors—all sorts of things. And there's one plaque for Teacher of the Year."

LeeAnn said, "Oh, yeah . . . I've seen that. Mrs. Palmer—my teacher in third grade—well, she won it last year."

Cara shook her head. "No, that's the new plaque. I'm talking about the *old* one, way back in the corner of the case. The teachers and the PTA have been giving that award for over twenty-five years. And about fifteen years ago, guess whose name got carved on that plaque?"

"Him?" asked LeeAnn. The bus was stopping at Edgewater Village. LeeAnn got up to let Cara into the aisle.

Cara nodded. "Yup. Mr. Karl Larson—Teacher of the Year, *three years in a row*." Cara heaved her backpack up onto one shoulder. As she headed for the door she looked back at the three kids staring after her, and she said, "Now *that's* what I call *news*."

CHAPTER 4

MISSING TEACHER FOUND IN NEARBY SUBURB

IT WAS A LONG drive home for Mr. Larson that Friday afternoon.

He was angry. Angry at that Landry girl. Angry at life in general, but most of all, angry at himself.

He'd been a teacher for almost twenty years now, and he couldn't remember the last time he had gotten mad in front of a class. All his talk about respect for one another, respect for different opinions, respect for honesty and real learning. Talk, talk, talk. All his words flew back into his face as he drove south on Interstate 55. Above the half-harvested cornfields on either side of the road, the flat gray sky was a good mirror for his thoughts.

Well . . . what about that little girl's respect for *him*? Mr. Larson tried to build a case for himself, tried to find a way to let himself off the hook for losing control. But he had to face facts. He knew Cara Landry had only been telling the truth. That was the hardest thing for him to admit.

By the time he drove into Williston, then down Ash Street and into his driveway, he was feeling a little better.

But when he opened the kitchen door and stepped into the empty house, the self-pity kicked in again. He opened the refrigerator and poured himself a tall glass of cider. He walked into the living room and slumped into the big armchair.

"What do those kids know about me, anyway?" he thought. "What gives that Landry girl the right to judge me?"

Mr. Larson remembered his own fifth-grade teacher, Mrs. Spellman. She had been perfect. Her clothes and hair and lipstick were always just so. Her classroom was always quiet and orderly. She never raised her voice—she never had to. She wrote in that flawless cursive, and a little gold star on a paper from Mrs. Spellman was like a treasure, even for the toughest boys.

Then young Karl Larson saw Mrs. Spellman at the beach on Memorial Day with her family. She was sitting under an umbrella, and she wore a black swimsuit that did not hide any of her midriff bulges or the purple veins on her legs. Her hair was all straggly from swimming, and without any makeup or lipstick she looked washed out, tired. She had two kids, a girl and a boy, and she yelled at them as they wrestled and got sand all over the beach towels. Her husband lay flat on his back in the sun, a large man with lots of hair on his stomach, and it wasn't a small stomach. As Karl stood there staring, Mrs. Spellman's husband lifted his head off the sand, turned toward his wife, pointed at the cooler, and said, "Hey Mabel, hand me another cold one, would you?"

Karl was thunderstruck, and he turned and stumbled back to where his own family had set up their picnic on the beach. This big, hairy guy looked at *his* Mrs. Spellman and said, "Hey Mabel." At that moment, Karl Larson realized that the Mrs. Spellman he knew at school was mostly a fictional character, partly created by him, and partly created by Mrs. Spellman herself. The students and . . . and *Mabel* created Mrs. Spellman together, in order to do the job—the job of schooling.

As Karl Larson sat there sipping cider, he considered the Mr. Larson that Cara Landry and the rest of the class knew. They had no idea who Karl Larson was. They didn't know that he was the first person in his family who had ever gone to college. They didn't know about the sacrifices he and his parents had made so he could get an education, and how proud he had been to get his first job teaching school in Carlton over nineteen years ago.

They probably didn't know that his wife was a teacher too—eighth grade English at a school on Chicago's South Side. The kids had no idea how much Karl Larson had hated seeing his wife's job get harder and harder over the years. Barbara Larson worried day and night about whether she could ever make a real difference in the lives of those kids she loved so much. Her school had always been a pretty rough place, but now . . . now there were metal detectors at the doors, and an armed guard escorted teachers to a padlocked parking lot at the end of each school day.

These kids didn't know that he and his wife had two daughters, a sophomore and a senior at the University of Illinois. Both girls were happy there, good students, doing well. But each of them had been accepted at top-notch colleges in Connecticut and Ohio and California, and each had chosen to go to the state school because that was the college their parents could afford. And Karl Larson couldn't forgive himself.

How could fifth-graders understand how hard it had been for him and his wife to take care of their aging parents over the past eight years—first hers and now his? The kids didn't know, they couldn't know.

So here he was. It was a Friday afternoon, and he was sitting alone in a dark house, waiting for his wife to fight her way home through the rush-hour traffic. After about fifteen minutes he finally gathered enough energy to get up and go to the kitchen and start cooking supper.

Later, after dinner, Mr. Larson told his wife about the editorial. He was expecting some sympathy, but he should have known better. His wife was much too honest for that. It was one of the things he loved best about her. Barbara Larson leaned across the kitchen table and squeezed his arm and said, "Sounds like this little girl is looking for a teacher, Karl—that's all. She's just looking for a teacher."

Mr. Larson tried to remember when he had stopped being a good teacher. But it wasn't like there was one particular moment you could point to. Teachers don't burn out all at once. It happens a little at a time, like the weariness that can overtake a person walking up a steep hill—you begin to get tired and you slow down, and then you feel like you just have to stop and sit and rest.

And that's how Karl Larson felt—overburdened and depressed. Some mornings he could barely get out of bed, and now this . . . this *editorial*. It didn't seem fair to be judged this way.

But still, could he blame anyone but himself? Were those kids *supposed* to know anything about him? Should anything outside of the classroom even matter to them? Should it have mattered to young Karl Larson that Mrs. Spellman was also this lady named Mabel who had a beer-drinking husband with a large hairy stomach? No. At school, Mabel was Mrs. Spellman, and she was a good teacher.

Karl Larson could see it clearly. The only reason

that he and those kids were together was to do the job—the job of schooling. The kids didn't need Karl Larson's life story. They needed *Mr. Larson*, the teacher.

So, over the weekend Karl Larson gradually faced the facts. *The Landry News* had told the truth. Mr. Larson the teacher was guilty as charged.

And Karl Larson knew he had to do something about it.

CHAPTER 5

HOMEWORK: HARD BUT IMPORTANT

WHEN CARA FINISHED taping it back together late Friday afternoon, she left the first edition of *The Landry News* on the kitchen table and went to her bedroom. She wanted to find the stack of newspapers she had made during fourth grade. When she came back with the small pile of earlier editions, her mother was standing at the table, reading the editorial about Mr. Larson.

Looking up, her mother said, "Let me guess: The teacher tore this up after he read it, right?"

Cara nodded.

"Cara, honey, you have done it this time." Her mother scanned the patchwork newspaper and heaved a long, tired sigh. "Well, at least this is the only copy and Mr. Larson didn't run it down the hall to the principal—like some other teachers have done."

Mrs. Landry dropped heavily onto one of the chairs beside the table. She looked at her daughter standing there. "Now tell me, Cara: Are you angry at me? Is that why you do this? Because if you are trying to hurt me, I just want to tell you that it's working. It's working just great."

Tears welled up in her mother's eyes, and Cara looked at her, unblinking. "No, Mother, I am not trying to hurt you. And you shouldn't be upset. This is just a newspaper. These are just facts, Mother."

"Facts? Just look right here, young lady." Joanna Landry stabbed a red fingernail at the editorial. "This is not just *facts*. You have unloosed your acid little tongue on this man and said mean and hurtful things here."

Cara flinched at the accusation, but she jumped to defend herself. "It's an *editorial*, Mother, so it's *allowed* to have opinions in it. And all the opinions are based on facts. I didn't make any of that up. I never have made anything up. I just report the facts. *You* are the one who taught me to always tell the truth, remember? Well, I'm just telling the truth here."

Mrs. Landry was outgunned, and she knew it. It had been years since she had won an argument with Cara, and she wasn't going to win this one. But having to admit that her daughter was only telling the truth did not make things any easier. Here they were only one month into a new school year in a new town, and Cara was already stirring the pot, stewing up trouble. Joanna Landry could feel her hair getting grayer by the minute.

She took a deep breath. "You may *call* it just telling the truth, but ever since your father left, you have gone out of your way to tell the truth in the most *hateful* way you know how. And it just makes me sad, Cara. It's not fair to me, and it's bad for you, and it just makes me *sad*." And with that, Mrs. Landry stood up and went to her room and closed the door.

Cara's thin shoulders hunched together as she sat on the dinette chair, looking at the paper, waiting for the sobs to begin in her mother's bedroom. *She's wrong*, thought Cara. *This time, she's wrong.*

But last year, it was like her mother said. Cara *had* been hateful—to everyone. When her dad left, Cara was sure it was because of her. Her mom and dad had always argued about money and about saving for Cara's college and about buying Cara better clothes, about taking Cara on a nice vacation. When her father left and filed for divorce, she thought it was because he didn't want to feel responsible for a family—for her.

It was just bad timing that turned Cara into an outlaw journalist. The week her father moved out, Cara's fourth-grade teacher had begun a unit on newspapers, and Cara seized hold of the idea with murder in her heart. She became a ferocious reporter—aloof, remote, detached. She turned a cold, hard eye on her classmates and teachers, saw their weaknesses and silliness, and used her strong language skills to lash out. She stuck close to the truth, but the truth wasn't always pretty.

When she learned that a rather large teacher kept a desk drawer filled with candy bars and fatty treats, Cara wrote an editorial with the title, "Let's Chat about Fat." The story got some laughs, but it was too mean, almost cruel. It did not win Cara any new friends, and it sent all her old friends ducking for cover.

When she noticed that the cafeteria staff would sometimes carry home leftovers at the end of the day, Cara blew the whistle in a banner headline: FOOD WORKERS PERFORM DISAPPEARING ACT. But she hadn't done enough research. What they were doing was all legal and approved. The practice actually saved the school money by decreasing the garbage-disposal expenses. The principal made Cara go and apologize to the cafeteria workers. After that she thought it best to bring bag lunches to school.

Every week, somewhere in the school, Cara would put up the newest edition of *The Landry News*, and then wait for the consequences. After the story about the cafeteria workers, her research got more careful, and she was always sure of her facts. But the way she told her news stories was always designed to create a stir and get a reaction, and she was never disappointed. There were conferences with her mother and the principal, conferences with the principal and the school psychologist, and conferences with her mother and every one of her teachers. And every conference would then become the subject of a sarcastic editorial, published in the very next edition of *The Landry News*.

The only person who never showed up at a conference was the only person Cara really wanted to see: her dad.

Now as Cara sat at the kitchen table looking through the sheaf of fourth-grade editions, she had trouble imagining herself writing all this. So much anger. But this newest paper wasn't like the ones she had made last year. She was still sad, but she wasn't angry anymore. Things were better now.

Over the summer, she had started getting letters from her dad. He worked in Indianapolis now, and he had promised Cara that she could come and visit him there—maybe at Thanksgiving or Christmas. And he would be coming to Chicago pretty often, too. He had called to tell her he was sorry about the way things had worked out. He explained why he and her mom had split up. And it didn't have anything to do with her. Cara could see that now, and she could believe it was true, even if all the rest of it still didn't make any sense to her.

Cara tiptoed to her mother's door and listened. It was quiet. She knocked softly and her mom said, "Come on in, honey."

Her mom was on the bed, sitting with her back against the headboard. Her old leather-bound Bible lay open on her lap. There were some wadded tissues on the bedspread, and Joanna Landry swept them aside and patted the bed. Cara sat on the edge and took her mother's hand.

"Mom, I'm not writing the news because I'm angry. Honest. I'm really not mad anymore. I was. I was real mad last year, and I know I hurt a lot of people's feelings, and I'm sorry about that now. And I guess I should have stopped to think before I wrote this new editorial . . . and I'll tell Mr. Larson I'm sorry—I will. But I still think it's okay to tell the truth, and to publish it, too. I *like* being a reporter. It's something I'm *good* at, Mom."

Her mother reached for a fresh tissue with her free hand and dabbed at her eyes. "Cara honey, you know I just want the best for you, that's all. I just don't want you to make things hard for yourself. I feel so bad already—about me and your dad, I mean. I know that's been tough on you, and you took it so hard. But it wasn't anything to do with you. Can you see that?"

Cara nodded. "I know. It just felt that way, that's all. And I'm sorry I gave you so much more to worry about, Mom. But . . . but don't you think it'll be all right to keep on making my newspaper—if I'm careful, and if I only report the truth?"

Her mom smiled. "Listen to this, Cara. It's from the book of Psalms."

Joanna Landry and her daughter, Cara, discussing truth and mercy in their home in Carlton, Illinois.

MERCY AND TRUTH ARE MET TOGETHER;
RIGHTEOUSNESS AND PEACE HAVE KISSED
EACH OTHER.
TRUTH SHALL SPRING OUT OF THE EARTH;
AND RIGHTEOUSNESS SHALL LOOK DOWN
FROM HEAVEN.

Her mother smiled at her and said, "Truth is good, and it's all right to let the truth be known. But when you are publishing all that truth, just be sure there's some mercy, too. Then you'll be okay."

At that quiet moment, safe at home, it all sounded so simple to Cara Landry. But the test would come on Monday.

CHAPTER 6

TOP STRESS CAUSE FOR KIDS? ONE WORD: *FEAR*

AS CARA SAT in health class on Monday afternoon, she was sweating. She never sweated, not even during gym. But this wasn't a hot sweat. It was a dry, sticky-mouthed sweat. A scared sweat.

It was also a mad-at-herself sweat. Cara hated feeling like a coward. She fumed at herself. "But that's what I am: a big, fat coward."

Her mom had dropped her off at school early that morning. Cara had wanted to be there before the other kids arrived. She wanted to give a note to Mr. Larson.

Cara had spent most of Sunday night working on the note. She had ripped up about twenty pieces of paper trying to get it right. She practically knew it by heart:

Dear Mr. Larson:

    I want to say I'm sorry for the part of *The Landry News* that was about you. Maybe I should not have surprised you by just sticking it up on the wall like that for everyone else to read. It's just that I like making newspapers. I try to print only what's true, but I guess sometimes I don't think enough about how that can make people feel.

    I mean, I still think that what I said was pretty true, but I didn't mean to make you mad like that. So, I'm sorry.

        Sincerely yours,
        Cara L. Landry

At seven-thirty that morning Cara had been on her way through the halls, her shoes squeaking on the newly waxed floors. Cara had the note in her hand. She turned the corner, and there he was, coming out of room 145. As he turned to go the other way, toward the teachers' room, Cara wanted to call out, "Hey, Mr. Larson!" and then run right over, smile a little, and hand him the note. Instead she turned to stone, and her tongue stuck to the roof of her mouth. She flattened up against the lockers, then backed around the corner, making sure her rubber soles didn't squeak. She jammed the note into the pocket of her dress and ran out the nearest door to the playground.

All day long she had skulked around, making sure that wherever she was, Mr. Larson wasn't. LeeAnn had come with Betsy Lowenstein and three other girls to sit with her at lunch, and Cara had hardly said three words, she was so mad at herself. She just sat there like an idiot, chewing on her lower lip, and nodding and smiling once in a while as LeeAnn went on and on about how mad Mr. Larson had been on Friday.

But in ten minutes, there would be no escape. Unless . . . no. If she went to the nurse, the nurse would call her mom at her office, so that wouldn't work. And if she didn't go to class, then Mr. Larson would know she was a coward, and Joey DeLucca and LeeAnn Ennis would know she was a coward. And worst of all, Cara thought, "*I* would know that I am the biggest, fattest, weakest, lamest, chickenest *coward* who ever lived."

So when the bell rang, Cara Landry, the secret coward with the cold sweats, put on her bravest face and walked like a robot down the hall and into room 145.

CHAPTER 7

FANS BRACE FOR GRUDGE MATCH

AS THE BELL rang someone else was sweating. The tall man in the rumpled sport coat hunched lower in his chair, holding his newspaper a little higher than usual. He was staring at the batting averages, but he saw nothing except the image of a little girl in a brown plaid skirt, scared out of her wits, biting her lower lip. This was the same image he had seen all weekend long. And now that little girl would be in his classroom again, the room where he was supposed to be the teacher. Mr. Larson reached for his thermos for the tenth time that day and remembered for the tenth time that it contained nothing but last Friday's coffee, as cold as the palms of his hands and as bitter as his churning stomach.

The kids came in and immediately began pulling the jumbled desks into rows. A room somehow feels safer with the desks all lined up. Everyone sat down. There was no goofing off, no loud talking like there had been at the start of class on Friday. It was the same teacher reading his newspaper, same kids, same room. But everything was different, and everyone knew it. And Cara Landry knew it best.

Cara sat as close as she could to the door at the back of the room. She wasn't really thinking about it, but somewhere on the edge of her mind she wanted to be ready for a quick getaway. She stared at her library book, reading the same paragraph over and over and over. When the bell rang, she jumped at the sound and quickly looked around to see if anyone had seen her jump. Joey DeLucca had been watching her, and he smiled and gave her a thumbs up. Cara tried to smile back but shivered instead, and forced her eyes back to the safety of the open book on her desk. Her note to Mr. Larson was tucked inside the front of the book. She gripped the cover tightly, as if trying to keep her apology trapped there, afraid it might leap out and throw itself into Mr. Larson's hands.

Mr. Larson cleared his throat, noisily folded his paper, and stood up, still holding the rumpled sheets. Right away he wished he hadn't stood up. He felt so tall, towering alone up at the front of the classroom. Some of the kids looked at him, but just as many kept their eyes elsewhere, and the little girl in the brown plaid skirt and the white-collared shirt stared at her book, her knuckles white. Mr. Larson noticed she was reading *Incident at Hawk Hill*, and his mind tried to recall the plot, searching for some hidden meaning in Cara's choice of that particular book. He shook that thought away, like a pitcher shaking off a bad signal from a catcher.

Clearing his throat again, he said, "How many of you looked at a Sunday paper this weekend?" Timidly, almost all the kids raised their hands.

Without taking her eyes off her book, Cara raised her hand, too. She always read the Sunday *Chicago Tribune*, and the Sunday *Sun Times*. And if she could get her mom to pay for it at the newsstand on the way home from church, she read *The New York Times*, too. The Sunday papers were Cara's favorite part of the weekend.

Mr. Larson said, "How many of you looked at the *Chicago Tribune*?"

Over half of the same hands went up again.

"Fine—hands down. Now, how many of you read a part of the *Tribune other* than the comics?"

That question thinned out the crowd. Only four kids kept their hands up: Cara and Joey and two other boys. Cara looked up from her book, just for a second, glancing at Mr. Larson. He wasn't looking at her, but she could tell he had just looked away. And in that instant, Cara knew where these questions were heading.

Mr. Larson continued, "Now. How many of you read something other than the comics and the sports section in the *Tribune*?" Joey and the two other guys lowered their hands, and now only Cara had her hand up. Her face was pale, and her lips were pressed into a thin line, but she kept her hand up.

"You can put your hand down, Cara," said Mr. Larson. "But tell me, can you remember any particular story you read in the *Tribune*?"

To the rest of the class, it seemed like an accident that Mr. Larson was talking to Cara now, having a normal student-to-teacher, question-and-answer session. But it wasn't an accident at all. Mr. Larson knew that, and he knew from the expression on Cara's face that she knew it, too.

Cara looked right at Mr. Larson now, and looking at him made her feel better. He wasn't mad at her, Cara could tell. Mr. Larson wasn't angry, and he was just as uncomfortable as she was, as scared as everyone in the class. It was as if the whole class had taken a deep breath and held it. And now they were starting to exhale, Cara first.

Lowering her hand, Cara spoke carefully, at first with a little tremor in her voice. "I remember all the stories I read in the *Tribune*. The lead story on page one was about the meeting on the Middle East crisis, the second lead story was about the murder rate in Chicago compared to New York City, and then there were about three other smaller stories, including one about the oldest horse on the Chicago police force."

Mr. Larson raised his eyebrows, wrinkling his forehead. "You say you remember *all* the stories you read? Did you read the whole first section of the paper?"

Cara nodded.

"How about the Arts and Living section?"

Another nod.

"Finance? . . . Travel?"

Cara nodded, then nodded again.

"So what you're saying," said Mr. Larson, "is that basically, you read the entire *Chicago Tribune* this Sunday?"

The kids in the class had been following this exchange like a crowd watching a tennis match, their eyes going from one player to the other. All eyes were on Cara. In a steady, clear voice she said, "Well, maybe not every word in the whole paper—but yes, I read the whole thing."

With his eyes locked on hers, Mr. Larson said, "How about . . . the *editorials*?"

The whole class stopped breathing again. But Cara didn't miss a beat. If Mr. Larson wanted to play twenty questions about the newspaper, she wasn't going to back down and freeze up. "Editorials?" Cara said. "I always read the editorials. It's the part of the paper I like the best, so I save it for last. Some people like to save . . . the *sports* section for last. But I like the editorials."

As Cara said "the sports section," Mr. Larson almost flinched. *Phew—this one doesn't miss a thing!* he thought to himself. Out loud he said, "And why do *you* like the editorials so much, Cara?"

Cara was all set to say, "Because an editor can speak right up and tell the world if someone is being *lazy* or *stupid* or *crooked* or *mean*." Those biting words were already forming in her mouth. But then she remembered what her mom had said on Friday night—about always telling the truth but adding some mercy.

And in that heartbeat of a moment between the thought and the spoken word, it struck Cara that Mr. Larson didn't have to be doing or saying any of this. He could have just walked into class, poured himself a cup of coffee, and hidden behind his newspaper all afternoon. Why was he asking her all these questions? And then Cara saw it. Mr. Larson was being a teacher. He was telling her that her editorial had been correct—truthful. And now Mr. Larson was giving Cara a chance to add a little mercy, if she wanted to.

Mr. Larson prompted her, "You like the editorials because . . . why?"

Cara took another few seconds, choosing her words with great care. "Because it's where the newspaper can say the things that are hard to say, and it's where the newspaper apologizes if it makes a mistake. It's where you get to see the heart of the newspaper."

Mr. Larson smiled, and his pale eyebrows went up as he said, "The *heart* of the newspaper? I didn't know newspapers had hearts."

Cara couldn't help smiling a little herself, and she

said, "Only the *good* newspapers have hearts."

"Hmmm." That's all Mr. Larson said. Just, "Hmmm," and their conversation was over.

Mr. Larson took three steps back, and bending over a little, he patted the stack of newspapers beside his desk. "These old papers aren't good for much, so I want each of you to take one or two of them, and find the editorials. Clip them out, read them, pass them around, compare them. And then see what kind of . . . what kind of a heart you think the *Sun Times* or the *Tribune* has. Write down what you think, and then maybe the class can talk about it in a couple of days."

And with that, Mr. Larson sat down in his chair and opened up his paper. With his eyes on the sports page, he reached for his thermos, and poured some of Friday's cold coffee into a cup. He wasn't planning on drinking any of it, but he wanted things to look and feel normal again.

A line formed as some of the kids came up to get old newspapers. The tension in the classroom was gone, and the familiar hum of noise returned, increasing rapidly. Cara immediately stood up, dragged a desk into her back corner, and pulled the map tripod over behind her. She sat down in her makeshift office, her heart racing.

And she smiled. Mr. Larson wasn't mad at her, and she had gotten to apologize to him, sort of. She also smiled because the whole class had an assignment, the first real assignment Mr. Larson had given since school started.

But it was more than that. Cara smiled because she had just gotten an idea, a new idea for her editorial in the next edition of *The Landry News*.

CHAPTER 8

VOLUNTEERS LINE UP FOR DANGER

IF THE PRINCIPAL had walked past Mr. Larson's doorway on that Monday, he would have thought it was just another out-of-control afternoon in Larsonland. But in fact, the room was filled with focused activity. It looked like chaos, but the kids were doing an assignment. Sprawled on the floor, standing around in small groups, or sitting on desktops, they were leafing through old newspapers, looking for the editorial pages. And as they flipped through the wide sheets of newsprint, kids kept finding all the other odds and ends that fill up a big city newspaper.

LeeAnn called out, "Hey Sharon, I just found a story about a lady in Cicero who died and left her house to her Siamese cat—I'm not kidding—to her *cat*. Look . . . there's a picture. This cat owns a house!"

Steven had been reading an article about some new animals being added to the Brookfield Zoo, and now he was arguing with Alan about which was more dangerous: a lion or a black rhinoceros.

Phil was reading the obituaries, and every few minutes he discovered a person who had the same last name as a kid in the class. Then he'd call out things like, "Hey, Tommy. Did you have a relative named Kasimir who owned a bakery in Glen Ellyn? The guy died in a car crash on Saturday."

Some kids had actually found the editorial pages and were now hunting around the classroom, searching for scissors and tape and glue and construction paper.

Cara wasn't doing the assignment. She was going to, of course, just not right now. She was working on something more important: the second edition of *The Landry News*. A spiral notebook was open on the desk in front of her, and she was making a list of possible lead stories.

Joey tapped at the bulletin board behind Cara as if it were the door to a room. "Knock, knock," he said. "Anybody here?"

The sound startled Cara. She swung around in her chair, annoyed at the interruption, but when she saw it was Joey, her mind went almost blank for a moment. Then Cara smiled and said, "Sure, I'm here."

Joey grinned and leaned one shoulder up against the wall. "So what do you think?" he asked, his voice lowered. "What's up with Larson? Is he crazy or what? I thought he would still be mad."

Cara nodded. "So did I, but he really wasn't. It's kind of weird, because now he knows that we're all thinking about what kind of a teacher he is. I think he's just trying to figure out what to do next. And did you notice that we all have an *assignment*—a real assignment?"

Joey rolled his eyes and wrinkled his nose. "Yeah, I noticed—everybody noticed. Thanks a lot, little miss newspaper girl." Then with a devilish grin Joey said, "And Mr. Larson didn't say a thing about *The Landry News*—like 'You'd better not say anything else about me,' or 'You can just forget about making another newspaper.' So are you going to?"

Cara looked at Joey like he was crazy. "Make another one? Did you think I *wasn't* going to? Of course I'm going to make another edition!"

Joey pushed off the wall and held up his hands as if Cara had jumped toward his throat. "Hey, hey—just asking, that's all. I figured you would. Everyone's gonna be watching for it, and not just the kids in this class, either. You know Ted Barrett on the red team? Well, I told him about what happened on Friday, and he said for me to be sure to tell him when your next paper comes out."

Cara was flattered, but her smile turned to a frown. She said, "But I only make one copy of the newspaper, and I'm going to put it up on the wall in here, and we're on the blue team—so how's Ted even going to see it?"

"Duh—," said Joey. "Ever hear of something called a

computer?" He pointed to the two computer workstations on the other side of the classroom. Ellen Rogers was using the encyclopedia on one of them, and David Fox sat at the other, headphones clamped on his head, playing some sort of geography game. Joey said, "You make your newspaper on a computer, and then you can print up as many copies as you want. Simple."

"I . . . I don't really know how to use a computer," stammered Cara, blushing. "At least not well enough for something like this. We . . . I don't have one at home, and the school where I used to live only had a couple of computers, and no one ever let me get near them. I think I had a . . . a bad reputation there."

"A bad reputation?" Joey grinned. "You? Hmmm. Let me guess . . . could that have had something to do with making newspapers?" Then he went on seriously, "But really, it's not hard to use a computer. I talked with Ed, and we want to be on your staff, you know, like work for the newspaper. You can do your writing right here in the classroom, or anywhere. Ed and me, we're really good with the computers down in the resource center—those are the newest ones in the school. And as long as a teacher says it's okay, Ms. Steinert will let us use the whole setup—printers, paper, everything. What do you think?"

Cara hesitated. She wasn't expecting this. *The Landry News* was *her* newspaper, something she did all by herself.

Still, this offer was something to think about. If she kept on making just one copy by hand, yes, she could keep total control of it. But with only one copy, not many kids would ever get to read the *News*. And as Mr. Larson had proved, making only one copy means that it only takes one angry reader to shut off the whole circulation instantly.

Cara thought about what she had said to her mom. It was true. She wasn't making *The Landry News* now because she was angry. She was making it because she was good at it, because she liked being a reporter and a newswriter. She was determined to be a good journalist, and every good journalist knows that circulation is important.

And besides all that, it was Joey DeLucca standing here smiling at her, offering to help. So Cara made a decision.

She smiled at Joey and stood up. She said, "Sounds good. Let's ask Mr. Larson if we can go and talk to Ms. Steinert right now."

A minute later Mr. Larson looked at Joey and Cara over the top of his newspaper. "The library?" he said. "You want to go to the library?"

Joey nodded. "We need your permission to use the computers there for a . . . a project."

Mr. Larson looked from Joey's face to Cara's. Without showing any approval or disapproval, he lay

Karl Larson listens closely as Cara and Joey DeLucca ask permission to work on a "project."

down his paper, pulled open the top drawer of his desk, and found a memo pad with his name on the top. He picked up a pen and said, "What's the date?"

Cara said, "October eighth."

As Joey and Cara watched, Mr. Larson started writing, saying the words out loud as he did. "Dear Ms. Steinert—Joey DeLucca and Cara Landry have my permission to use the resource-center computers for a . . ."

Mr. Larson lifted his pen off the paper and looked up at Cara, and then at Joey. Then he wrote the last word, and said, "For a . . . project." He added his initials below the sentence, tore the memo from the pad, and folded it in half.

Handing the note to Cara, Mr. Larson said, "Hope this project is a good one."

Cara nodded and said, "Oh, it is. It's a good one."

"Well," said Mr. Larson, "you'll have to tell me all about it one of these days." As he dropped the memo pad into his drawer and opened up his newspaper again, Mr. Larson said, "Please be sure you're both back here five minutes before the last bell."

Looking over the top of his reading glasses, Mr. Larson watched Cara and Joey walk quickly out the classroom door.

And sitting there behind his newspaper, Mr. Larson grinned.

CHAPTER 9

K-9 UNIT SNIFFS SUSPICIOUS ACTIVITIES

LATE IN THE DAY on that same Monday afternoon, all the kids were gone, and the school was quiet. Mr. Larson had picked up his briefcase, his red thermos, and his raincoat, and he was headed toward the back door of the school. As usual, he walked past the window wall in front of the resource center. Through the glass he saw Ms. Steinert pushing a cart of books.

She looked up as he was going past, and Mr. Larson nodded and gave a friendly smile. But when Ms. Steinert saw him, she stopped in her tracks and waved excitedly, motioning him to come inside. She trotted over and met him at the door.

"Karl, I'm so glad I caught you! This journalism project you are doing with your afternoon group?— it sounds sooo *in*teresting—but I just wanted to give you a heads-up about the possible extra expenses."

Mr. Larson thought, *Journalism project? What journalism project?!* He was surprised, but he didn't let it show. He just asked, "Expenses? Expenses for what?"

Ms. Steinert said, "Now before you get all worried, just let me say that Joey DeLucca is a *very* trustworthy young man, and I *know* that he will not be wasting *any* materials. But the children *have* asked to use the big printer and the eleven-by-seventeen paper, and *that's* an extra expense. However, I really agree with them that if it's going to feel like a *real* newspaper, it needs to be on a large sheet, don't you think so, too? Now, the little Landry girl said that eventually they will want to be printing on *both* sides of the paper, and that can be pretty hard on the toner cartridges and the imaging rollers—so *that's* another possible expense."

Katherine Steinert had always reminded Mr. Larson of a schnauzer—the kind of small dog that runs around and around in circles, yipping and jumping up and chasing its tail. Her close-cropped, gray-and-white curly hair added to this impression. Ms. Steinert talked so fast that she often seemed to be panting. Mr. Larson admired her energy and enthusiasm, but talking with her always made him feel tired. He wanted to ask her what Cara and Joey had said about this newspaper they wanted to print, but before he could get a sentence started, she was talking again.

"Now, as you *know* from the memo that Mr.—I mean *Dr*. Barnes sent around at the start of the school year, the office is now tracking expenses for supplies and materials. You'll recall that the principal said they are tracking the expenses by grade, by team, and also by teacher. Each teacher and each team is allotted so much credit for each semester, and then, if you haven't used up your credits before . . ."

Mr. Larson nodded and smiled, but he was lost. The details of school administration were not one of his strong points, and Ms. Steinert was talking too fast anyway. But he waited patiently for her to be done, because he wanted more information.

"So if you'll just step over to my desk," Ms. Steinert continued, "I have the requisition forms all ready for you to sign, and then your students can come in any-time and have what they need. It's *such* a good idea, and they are *sooo excited* about it."

Before she could take another breath, Mr. Larson blurted out, "Did they say when they wanted to have something ready to print?"

"Oh my, yes!" said Ms. Steinert. "Cara was con-vinced that they would have a paper all finished by *this* Friday—*imagine*—this *Fri*day! Of course, I expect it will be more like three weeks from now—but they were *sooo eager* to get going that I didn't have the heart to tell them that they are looking at an *awful* lot of work here. You know, kids underestimate things like this all the time. Why, just last week . . ."

Mr. Larson signed the expense forms. As Ms. Steinert went on talking about a South America project that a group of second-graders had just finished, Mr. Larson smiled and nodded and began backing toward the door. She walked right along with him, held the door open for him, and when he was all the way out in the hallway, Ms. Steinert finished up by saying, "And, Karl, I really do think this is a *won*derful idea you've had, and like I was saying, the kids should finish up a great little newspaper project in about three weeks or so—I'll be watching! Now, you have a safe drive home tonight, Karl."

Mr. Larson smiled, turned, and walked. He took several deep breaths. Finishing a conversation with Ms. Steinert always made him feel like he had just escaped from drowning.

As he walked along the familiar corridor, he thought over what Ms. Steinert had told him. It shouldn't have surprised him. When Cara and Joey left the room earlier to go use the computer, hadn't he known that their "project" would have something to do with Cara's newspaper? Of course he had. And hadn't he expected Cara to keep on publishing her newspaper? Absolutely.

There was only one thing Ms. Steinert had told him that Mr. Larson knew wasn't true. There was no way it would take three weeks to produce the next *Landry News*. If Cara Landry said she would be ready to print by Friday, then Friday it would be.

CHAPTER 10

NEW TEAM PICKS UP STEAM

JOEY HADN'T BEEN bragging. He really did know what he was doing with that new computer. The first time he and Cara went to the resource center on Monday afternoon, it took him only twenty minutes to set up the basic framework of the newspaper. Cara watched as the newspaper took shape in front of her eyes on the computer monitor. Joey selected the eleven-by-seventeen-inch paper size, and then across the top he typed THE LANDRY NEWS in ninety-point type. Seeing the name like that, large and crisp and clear, gave Cara a thrill. The finished paper would not be quite as large as the newspapers she had made by hand, but it would look much more real, more important. It was like a new beginning.

Joey showed Cara how she could choose different styles of type, and after trying five or six, she decided that the one called Palatino looked best for the name of the newspaper—clear and readable without being show-offy.

"Now we can draw some boxes where the columns will go," Joey explained. The paper is eleven inches wide . . . and there needs to be about a quarter-inch margin on both sides . . . so we have ten and a half inches to work with. How about five columns that are each two inches wide? That will leave an eighth of an inch between them." Almost as quickly as Joey said it, the columns appeared on the screen. He pointed at the lines around each column and said, "On the real paper, these lines won't be there, but we can leave them for now so you can see how much space there is to fill."

Cara gulped and said, "There's a *lot* of space to fill, isn't there."

"Well . . . yeah," Joey said, "but remember, there can be headlines and drawings and pictures and dingbats—they all take up space, too."

"Pictures?" asked Cara. "I can put *pictures* in the paper?"

"Yup," said Joey. "Pictures, drawings, cartoons—whatever you want." He pointed at a little machine on the table beside the monitor. "That thing is called a scanner. You can put a sheet into that slot, the scanner will make a copy of whatever's on it, then you can add it to the newspaper on the screen and print it out—bingo!"

Cara was feeling a little overwhelmed by all the choices. "So . . . so do I have to type up all my news stories on a computer now?" she asked.

"Well, someone does," said Joey. "But it doesn't really have to be you. If you like, write things down the way you want them, then me or Ed could type it up—or even someone else. Alan's real good at keyboarding, and so is Sarah. I bet they'd help out if you ask."

Joey turned back to the computer screen. "Now I'm going to print out a copy. Then you can use a pencil to sketch in where headlines should go . . . what pictures you want—whatever. I'll print out two copies. They'll be good for your planning."

A minute later, Joey handed Cara the sheets, still warm from the printer. Holding the actual pieces of paper, seeing the name large and clear across the top, Cara stopped worrying. She didn't understand all the computer stuff—not yet—but she understood paper. In the end it was just going to be a piece of paper—paper and ink and ideas.

With a big smile Cara looked up and said, "This is great, Joey."

And four days later, there it was—paper and ink and ideas. Joey DeLucca and Ed Thomson were standing at the doorway of room 145, handing out crisp, clean copies of *The Landry News*. It had not been easy, but they had made the Friday deadline.

The lead story was the results of a survey that Cara and LeeAnn had taken on Tuesday and Wednesday. They had asked seventy-five fifth-graders to name their favorite teacher at Denton Elementary School, and to explain their choice. The headline was: MRS. PALMER CHOSEN FAVORITE TEACHER.

There was a "Top-Ten List of the Least-Favorite Cafeteria Foods." The list ended with:

> And the number one least-favorite cafeteria food at
> Denton Elementary School—two words: creamed corn.

There was sports news about the recreation department basketball season, with the total wins and losses so far for each of the fifth-grade teams.

In the center of the page there was a picture of the boys' locker-room door. Ed had brought his dad's instant camera to take the picture, and Joey had scanned it in. The headline below the picture said HOLD YOUR NOSE! and the article was about why the locker rooms—boys' and girls'—smell so bad.

And of course there was an editorial.

As Ed and Joey handed out papers, Cara took a copy from the four or five papers she was keeping for herself and walked up to Mr. Larson's desk. He saw Cara coming out of the corner of his eye but kept reading the sports page until she said, "Mr. Larson?"

He said, "Yes? Oh—hi, Cara. What can I do for you?"

Cara was nervous. She held the copy of *The Landry*

News behind her back and, trying to smile, she said, "You know that project Joey and I wanted to go to the library for? Well, it's done, and I wanted to show it to you . . . here." And Cara handed him the newspaper.

Mr. Larson leaned forward across his desk to take it, acting surprised. "Project? Oh, yes . . . the project in the library." Looking over the newspaper quickly and then back up at Cara's face, he said, "Yes, I remember—I asked you if it was going to be a good project . . . What do you think? Are . . . are you happy with the way it turned out?"

Cara gulped and nodded. "Uh-huh. We had to work kind of quickly, and there's not all that much in it, but . . . but we like the paper, and I . . . and we just wanted you to have a copy."

"Well . . . thank you, Cara," said Mr. Larson, a little haltingly. "I'll enjoy reading this."

Cara nodded, smiled awkwardly, and said, "You're welcome," and backed away from Mr. Larson's desk. She turned and headed for her space in the back corner of the room.

Mr. Larson leaned back in his chair and held up *The Landry News* to get a better look at it. He really didn't know what to expect. As he scanned the page, his eye fell to the lower right-hand corner of the paper—to the editorial.

From the Editor's Desk
New Looks

The Landry News has a new look this week. A lot of people helped to make the improvements. Without Mr. Larson, Ms. Steinert, Joey DeLucca, Ed Thomson, LeeAnn Ennis, Sharon Gifford, and Alan Rogers, the changes and also some of this week's stories would not have been possible.

This paper has taken another new look this week, a look at what a newspaper is for. Above all, a newspaper has to tell the truth. Telling the truth can sometimes make people angry. Does that mean that a newspaper should try to stay away from a story that might bother someone? It all depends on the thought behind the newspaper—the newspaper's heart.

A mean-hearted newspaper tries to find out things that are bad, and then tries to tell the truth in a way that will hurt others. Newspapers can get famous that way, but they don't do much good—for anybody.

A good-hearted newspaper tries to tell the truth in a way that helps people understand things better. A good-hearted newspaper can tell the same story as a mean-hearted paper, but it tells the story in a different way because it's for a different reason.

As a reminder that *The Landry News* is trying to be a good-hearted newspaper, starting with the next edition, below the name of the paper, there will be a new motto: Truth and Mercy.

And that's the view this week from the *News* desk.

Cara Landry, Editor in Chief

Mr. Larson had started slowly swiveling his chair around toward the chalkboard when he was about halfway through the editorial. He could feel his eyes misting up, and he was pretty sure someone would be watching him while he read the paper. When Mr. Larson finished it, he smiled as he blinked hard, and he reached for his coffee to help gulp away the lump in his throat. He hadn't felt this good about being a teacher for a long, long time.

After a minute, Mr. Larson got up and walked back toward Cara's mini-office. Now it was Cara's turn to pretend she didn't see someone coming.

Looking down on her over the top of the tripod map, Mr. Larson said, "Excuse me, Cara . . . would you happen to have an extra copy of this newspaper? My wife's a teacher, too, and I just know she'd love to read this editorial. It's really a good piece of writing."

Beaming with pleasure, Cara said, "Sure . . . sure, Mr. Larson. Here's another copy."

The second edition of *The Landry News* was a big hit. All seventy-five copies had been distributed in less than six minutes.

And late Friday afternoon, one copy of *The Landry News* ended up on the desk of Dr. Philip K. Barnes, Principal.

CHAPTER 11

TREMORS POINT TO MAJOR QUAKE

A COPY OF the second edition found its way to the office because the principal's secretary, Mrs. Cormier, had found one on the floor in the hallway. She thought Dr. Barnes would enjoy reading the article about the best teachers.

Dr. Barnes sat down at his desk and read every word of the newspaper carefully, nodding and smiling now and then. This was good, clean fun—excellent writing, a fine learning experience. The bit about the top-ten least-favorite foods was cleverly done, and the story about favorite teachers was written in a very positive way. The writers didn't take any cheap shots. There was no foul language. There was no criticism of the school, the school administration, or school policies. There was nothing even a little bit controversial about the second edition of *The Landry News*.

But when Dr. Barnes read the editorial, his eyes

narrowed, and his heartbeat quickened. A scowl formed on his broad, fleshy face, and his nostrils flared and quivered. He reached for a red pen, took off the cap, and starting over, he read through the entire paper again, looking for a problem, any problem. But when he was done, he had only circled one item on the whole page. It was in the editorial. He had drawn a heavy red circle around one name: Mr. Larson.

Dr. Phillip Barnes, principal of Denton Elementary School.

Dr. Barnes had strong opinions about Mr. Larson. For the seven years Dr. Barnes had been the principal of Denton Elementary School, Mr. Larson had been a constant problem.

Dr. Barnes didn't *hate* Mr. Larson. That would be too strong a word—too emotional. This had nothing to do with feelings, he told himself. This was a matter of professionalism. Dr. Barnes *disapproved* of Mr. Larson because Mr. Larson did not behave *professionally*. For Dr. Barnes, education was serious business, and Mr.

Larson took his educational responsibilities too lightly.

Dr. Barnes opened his desk drawer and took out the key to the file cabinet where he kept the records about each teacher at Denton Elementary School. Swiveling around in his chair, he unlocked and opened the wide file drawer. It wasn't hard to find Mr. Larson's file. It was three times fatter than any other file in the drawer.

Every year Dr. Barnes got letters about Mr. Larson from worried parents. Parents asked if it was normal to have no homework in social studies, no homework in reading, and no homework in English—no homework *at all* for the *whole year*! Parents wrote to ask if their children could be transferred to the red team, and the real reason was always the same: getting out of Mr. Larson's class.

At the end of every school year each teacher was required to have a meeting with the principal. It was called a performance review. Dr. Barnes flipped through the stack of performance review sheets he had filled out for Mr. Larson—one for each of the last seven years. Poor. Poor. Unacceptable. Poor. Unacceptable. Unacceptable, and—Unacceptable.

At the bottom of each review form, there was room for a brief statement from the teacher. Over the past seven years, every statement from Mr. Larson had been pretty much the same. Turning to last year's review sheet, Dr. Barnes gritted his teeth and read what Mr. Larson had written:

It is clear that Phil and I have very different philosophies of education. I sadly acknowledge that he objects to some of my methods and practices.

Sincerely,

Karl A. Larson, Teacher

Many parents thought that Mr. Larson should not be a teacher. Several school board members thought that Mr. Larson should be fired, and several other board members thought it would be nice if Mr. Larson retired—early.

But as every principal and every school board knows, getting rid of a teacher is not an easy thing to do. There has to be something serious, something provable, something that violates school policies, or something that violates the law.

Dr. Barnes closed up Mr. Larson's fat file folder, put it back in the drawer, shut the cabinet, locked it, and dropped the key back into its place.

He set his copy of *The Landry News* in the center of his desk blotter. Then he laced his fingers behind his head and leaned back in his chair. He smiled. He had a good feeling about this little newspaper. This situation had possibilities. This could turn out to be just what a lot of people had been hoping for.

Sitting up suddenly, Dr. Barnes reached for his

phone. He punched Mrs. Cormier's extension. He could hear her bustling around behind him out in the main office area, no doubt getting ready to leave. He could have swiveled his chair around and talked to her, but he enjoyed using the phone. It seemed more official.

The phone on Mrs. Cormier's desk rang one, two, three, four times. She finally answered. "Yes, Dr. Barnes?" There was an edge to Mrs. Cormier's voice. It was four-fifteen on a Friday, and she was in no mood for secretary games. Standing at her desk with her coat and hat on, Mrs. Cormier could see Dr. Barnes sitting there, fifteen feet away, drumming on the desk with his fingers. Really—how hard could it be for him to just swing around, smile, and *talk*?

"Uh, yes . . . Mrs. Cormier, um . . . please put a note into Mr. Larson's box for me. I want to meet with him Monday, right after school—*right* after school. It's a matter of some importance."

Mrs. Cormier hung up her phone and called through the open door, "Monday is Columbus Day, Dr. Barnes. But I'll leave him a note about a meeting on Tuesday, and then I'll be going. Have a good long weekend, now."

Mrs. Cormier scrawled a hasty note onto a sheet of Dr. Barnes's stationery, stuffed it into Mr. Larson's mail slot, and was out the door in thirty seconds.

CHAPTER 12

GROWTH SPURT DOESN'T HURT

ON TUESDAY AFTERNOON Mr. Larson called the class to order. He wrote three words on the chalkboard, from left to right: Positive, Neutral, Negative.

Mr. Larson said, "An editorial writer has only got a little bit of space, so every word has to be chosen for power." Tapping the board as he said the key words, Mr. Larson continued, "The words a writer chooses can be positive, negative, or neutral. Is the writer building something up? That's positive writing. Tearing something apart? That calls for negative punches. And if the writer is just exploring, just looking all around an issue, that's a neutral treatment."

Cara raised her hand. Mr. Larson said, "Question, Cara?"

"But if an editor is taking a negative position on something like war or drugs, wouldn't that really be positive?"

Mr. Larson said, "Yes, and no. Yes, the *effect* might be

positive. But the *treatment*—the words themselves and the images they communicate—they would be negative. Now, everyone, look over the editorials you clipped. Let's get some lists going up here, positive, neutral, and negative."

For ten minutes the kids peppered Mr. Larson with words and phrases, and he wrote them down as quickly as he could.

The negative column filled up fastest with words like *stupid, disgraceful, foolish, laughable, wasteful, outraged, idiotic, scandalous, uninformed, half-baked, shamefully.*

Positive words and phrases included *generously, public-spirited, wise, beneficial, commendable, carefully researched, useful, honorable, good.*

Neutral words or phrases were a lot harder to find. In fact, the kids only found five: *apparently, clearly, not certain, understandably, presumably.* Then Mr. Larson led a rousing class discussion, more like a shouting match, about which kind of editorial treatment was best. Everyone finally agreed that there were times and places for all three kinds.

Reaching over to his desk, Mr. Larson grabbed a sheet of paper and taped it up onto the chalkboard. The class hushed. It was a copy of *The Landry News*.

"I know you've all seen this new and improved edition of *The Landry News*," he said. "And I know from the condition of the room and my shrinking newspaper stacks that you've all been looking at a lot of *other* newspapers, too." Mr. Larson smiled. "So give me some opinions. How is *The Landry News* different from the other papers you've been looking at—and how is it the same?"

No one said anything. "Come on, now, *we're* not being negative here, we're being neutral. In fact, we have every reason to be very positive." Pointing at the newspaper, he said, "This is quite a big change to happen in one week. I'm not asking for comments about the paper, just tell me—how is it *similar* to the other ones you've been reading, and how is it different . . . " Mr. Larson paused. "Who's got an idea? Ed? You must have an idea. Tell me a difference."

Ed gulped. Glancing at Cara and Joey before he spoke, he said, "Size? Our paper—I mean *The Landry News*—like, it doesn't have as many words?"

"Size! Excellent, Ed. Size." Mr. Larson wrote the word on the board. "Now someone else," said Mr. Larson, "another difference . . . LeeAnn?"

LeeAnn was ready. "Those other newspapers have hundreds of reporters and printers and stuff," she blurted out, "and this newspaper has only a few."

That broke things open. In just a few minutes, there was a long list of differences—things like advertisements, a purchase price, color pictures, comics, gossip columns, advice columns, world news.

Then came the list of similarities. It covered all the basics: *The Landry News* had local news stories, it had reporters, it had writers, it had a black-and-white picture, it had an editorial, it had readers, and it was interesting, just like the other papers.

Looking back and forth from list to list, Sharon raised her hand. Mr. Larson nodded at her. "Sharon?"

She said, "Well, why couldn't *The Landry News* have more of those other things in it, too, like columns and comics and stuff?"

"That's a fair question," said Mr. Larson, "but *I* can't answer it. You all missed another similarity that *The Landry News* has to those other papers. *The Landry News* also has an editor in chief, and if you've got a question about changing *The Landry News*, you'd have to ask her."

All eyes turned to Cara. She was sitting on a desk, one foot on the chair, the other leg crossed, her sharp little chin propped on her fist, with her elbow on her knee. She looked like that famous statue, *The Thinker*, but thin, with her brown plaid skirt covering her skinny knees and her ponytail flopped to one side.

She could feel the color rising in her cheeks. Mr. Larson was asking her to make the decision—Cara Landry, the editor in chief. The first thought that flashed through her mind was how much fun it would be to tell her mom about all this at supper tonight.

A lot had happened to Cara in the last ten days. Less than two weeks ago, Cara Landry had been the invisible girl. Now, every kid and every teacher in the school knew her name and her face. *The Landry News* used to be something Cara did completely on her own, something with a single voice and a single vision, an extension of her own thinking and her own two hands.

To make the newspaper that Mr. Larson had taped up there on the chalkboard, Cara had needed the hands and eyes and ears of others. She had made new friends, and they had all worked and laughed, then argued and thought, and then laughed again. She had seen how good it made all of them feel to make the newspaper together.

Cara didn't feel famous. What she felt was . . . useful. She felt needed. And she liked it.

And if just having four or five kids help with the paper could make it that much better and that much more fun, could it hurt to have the group get bigger?

Cara straightened up and looked around. Then she smiled—a warm, inclusive smile that made her whole face shine. And the editor in chief said, "If it's going to have more features, it's going to need more writers and reporters, more typists, more of everything. And it's not all that easy or fun—just ask LeeAnn or Joey! So whoever wants to help, come back to my desk. The deadline for the next edition is this Friday—and it's a short week!"

The whole class followed Cara back to her desk in the corner, and soon Joey and Ed and LeeAnn were helping Cara figure out how to divide up the work.

Left alone up at the front of the room, Mr. Larson turned around and slowly pulled his copy of *The Landry News* off the chalkboard. Sitting at his desk, he carefully peeled off the piece of tape. Then he pulled open the deep drawer on the bottom left, and took out a new file folder. With a green marker he wrote THE LANDRY NEWS on the tab in neat block letters. He folded the newspaper sheet exactly in half, put it into the file folder, and tucked it into the drawer.

By this time the noise in room 145 had reached a level that would have stunned, or possibly paralyzed, any other teacher at Denton Elementary School. But Mr. Larson heaved a satisfied sigh, poured himself a cup of hot coffee from his big red thermos, smiled, leaned back in his chair, and opened up his *other* newspaper to the sports section.

CHAPTER 13

STRONG WINDS IN FORECAST

MR. LARSON WAS on his way out of the building on Tuesday afternoon, briefcase in one hand, red thermos in the other, when he heard the unmistakable sound of Dr. Barnes's voice.

"Mr. Larson! Mr. Larson!" Dr. Barnes was trotting down the hall toward him, puffing, his face red.

Turning around, Mr. Larson managed to put a neutral expression on his face. He said, "Hi, Phil. How's it going?"

Dr. Barnes winced. He preferred to be called Dr. Barnes, or Principal Barnes. Mr. Larson always called him Phil.

"What are you doing?" Dr. Barnes asked incredulously.

"It's three-thirty—thought I'd go home for the night," said Mr. Larson.

Patting his forehead with a handkerchief, Dr. Barnes said, "Didn't you get my memo? We have a meeting today, right now, and you're fifteen minutes late."

"Hmmm," said Mr. Larson. "Guess I didn't get your note."

"But how could you have missed it? Mrs. Cormier put it in your mailbox on Friday afternoon. Didn't you get your mail this morning?"

Mr. Larson smiled and shrugged. "Guess not."

Dr. Barnes turned and motioned, and Mr. Larson began following him down the hall toward the office. Dr. Barnes said, "I'm glad I caught you. You're *supposed* to get your mail every morning, you know. Your mailbox is an important channel of faculty communication."

With a straight face, Mr. Larson said, "You know, I've heard that, Phil. But it's remarkable how many days I get by just fine without going to the office at all."

Dr. Barnes ignored this comment and opened the door that went directly into his office from the hallway. He held the door, letting Mr. Larson squeeze past him to go in first.

Shutting the door, Dr. Barnes motioned to the chair in front of his desk. Mr. Larson put his thermos and briefcase on the floor beside the chair, sat down, and crossed his long legs. It was not a comfortable chair. Mr. Larson wondered how many other squirming people had sat across from Principal Barnes this way. On the principal's desk was a prism of wood, engraved, PHILIP K. BARNES, B.A., M.ED., M.B.A., ED.D. On the paneled wall behind his chair, framed diplomas and certificates competed for space with photographs of Dr. Barnes shaking hands with important people, some of whom Mr. Larson could actually recognize. Ambition oozed from every photograph.

Dr. Barnes unfolded his copy of *The Landry News*, and slid it across the desk toward Mr. Larson. Mr. Larson saw his name there, circled in red ink. The principal said, "Tell me, Mr. Larson, what exactly is your involvement with this newspaper?"

Mr. Larson put on his reading glasses, looked down at the paper, and then up at Dr. Barnes. "I'm teaching a unit on journalism," said Mr. Larson, "and some of the kids in the class have started a newspaper—sort of as a project. It's good writing, don't you think?"

"Yes," said Dr. Barnes. "The writing is fine. That's not the problem."

"Problem?" said Mr. Larson. "I didn't know there was any sort of a problem. What problem are you talking about, Phil?"

Dr. Barnes leaned back in his chair and began gently swiveling from side to side, with his eyes staying steady on Mr. Larson's face. "Are you familiar with a Supreme Court decision known as the *Hazelwood* case?"

Mr. Larson immediately replied, "*Hazelwood?* Of course. In 1988 the United States Supreme Court ruled that school principals have the legal right to say what does or does not get printed in school newspapers. It was not a unanimous decision, but five justices agreed that a school principal has this authority. Some people think the Court's decision is a violation of the Constitution's guarantee of free speech. Others say that if the school is the publisher, the school gets to make the final decisions, just like the owner of a newspaper would."

Dr. Barnes was impressed. He had underestimated just how well read and well informed Mr. Larson was. Nodding, he said, "You have a clear grasp of the case, I see. And tell me, Mr. Larson, do you *agree* with the Court's decision?"

Mr. Larson smiled and said, "That's kind of like asking if I agree with the law of gravity. Whether I agree with it or not, it's still the law."

Dr. Barnes chuckled. "True, quite true. The law is the law, and since it is, then I assume you will not mind if I review each new edition of this paper before it is distributed, correct?"

Mr. Larson kept smiling, but there was no smile in his voice. He said, "If it was a *school* newspaper, I wouldn't mind that at all. But you see, Phil, it's not. *The Landry News* is a *classroom* newspaper. It's made by my students in room 145, and I have every confidence in their ability to decide what ought to be in it."

Leaning forward so that his stomach pressed against the desk, Dr. Barnes pointed at the newspaper. He said, "If this is a *classroom* newspaper, all the copies should have stayed in your classroom, Mr. Larson. Mrs. Cormier found this copy on the floor all the way over in the third-grade hallway."

"You know, it's a funny thing about paper," said Mr. Larson. "My wife and I once flew to New York City for a long weekend, and after we flew back to Chicago on Sunday night, we walked to our car, drove home, went inside, and then I sat down and put my feet up. And you know what? There was a piece of paper—an advertisement for a New York restaurant—stuck right onto the bottom of my shoe. Paper has a way of getting around."

Dr. Barnes did not appreciate the humor in Mr. Larson's story. Frowning, he patted the paper on his desk. "Do you know how many copies of this newspaper were printed?"

Mr. Larson shook his head, "No, I can honestly say I do not know how many copies the kids made. I left that up to them. They are proud of their work—and they have a right to be. I'm sure they've shared some copies with their friends, probably carried them home to show their folks, too."

"Seventy-five copies," said Dr. Barnes. "According to Ms. Steinert, your students made *seventy-five* copies of this newspaper. You have twenty-three students in your afternoon class, so unless you are trying to tell me that each child kept three or more copies, then this is a *school* newspaper. This newspaper is produced here, in

Dr. Barnes talks to Mr. Larson about the Hazelwood case.

my school, using school computers and school paper and school printers and school electricity and school time."

Mr. Larson was quiet for a moment. He resisted the urge to start yelling. He wasn't looking for a big fight with Philip Barnes—never had been. In many ways he admired the principal. Doc Barnes looked out for what he thought were the best interests of the kids. He tried to keep everyone happy and working together—the teachers and the parents and the school board and the superintendent—not an easy thing to do. Dr. Barnes was a good principal, a good administrator. But Dr. Barnes was not a good teacher. And Mr. Larson was dead certain that if Dr. Barnes got involved in *The Landry News*, something important would be lost.

Clearing his throat, Mr. Larson stood up. "Well, it's happened before, hasn't it, Dr. Barnes? This is just one more educational matter that you and I disagree about. *I* say that *The Landry News* is a *classroom* project. The paper and printers and computers and time and electricity are being used as a normal part of my work as a teacher in this school, just like any other teacher and any other group of kids doing any other project."

Dr. Barnes stood up, too, and tapping on the newspaper sheet with his index finger, he asked, "Then you take full responsibility for this newspaper and whatever is printed in it?"

"I sure do," said Mr. Larson. "Absolutely."

"Very well then," said Dr. Barnes mildly. "I guess our meeting is over."

Mr. Larson bent down to pick up his briefcase and his red thermos, and as he did, Dr. Barnes stepped out from behind his desk and pulled open the door to the hallway. As Mr. Larson stepped into the corridor, Dr. Barnes said, "Mr. Larson, will you please be sure that I get one copy of each new paper as it comes out? I'd like to keep informed about the progress of your . . . *classroom* project."

"Next edition comes out this Friday," said Mr. Larson. "We'll be sure to get you a copy. Have a good evening, Phil."

Closing the door that exited to the hall, Dr. Barnes walked over and opened the other door that went into the main office. "Mrs. Cormier—I need you to take a letter for me."

Mrs. Cormier looked up at the clock. It was three forty-three. "Be right there, Dr. Barnes." She grabbed her pad and a ballpoint, walked in, and sat where Mr. Larson had been.

Dr. Barnes paced slowly behind her and said, "This is a memorandum to the personnel file of Mr. Karl Larson. I have just concluded a meeting with Mr. Larson. We discussed a newspaper being produced by students in his afternoon class. It appears to be a school newspaper, and I have asked Mr. Larson to show each copy to me before publication so that any objectionable material can be removed before it is distributed. Mr. Larson has insisted that the newspaper is a classroom newspaper and has taken full responsibility for the contents of each edition. He has agreed to supply me with one copy of each new edition that he and his students publish."

Stepping over to look over Mrs. Cormier's shoulder, he asked, "Did you get all that?" Mrs. Cormier nodded. "Good," said Dr. Barnes. "I'd like three copies for signature sometime tomorrow. Thank you, Mrs. Cormier."

As she left his office, Dr. Barnes sat down again and swiveled slowly back and forth.

His meeting with Mr. Larson had not gone exactly as he had planned. But Dr. Barnes was happy with the results—very happy.

Mr. Larson had accepted full responsibility for the newspaper and everything in it.

The more Dr. Barnes thought about that, the better he liked it. All he had to do was wait. One mistake would drop Mr. Larson right into the frying pan.

CHAPTER 14

LAW FOR ALL, ALL FOR LAW

WHEN THE AFTERNOON class came whooping into room 145 on Wednesday, the kids were surprised to see a TV and a VCR on a cart next to Mr. Larson's desk. Mr. Larson had never showed videos to them before.

When everyone had quieted down, Mr. Larson said, "I know you all need to get right to work on the newspaper, but first I want you to watch something I taped on TV late last night."

He pushed the play button, and a talk-show host told a joke about the president and the vice president telling lies to each other. The TV audience laughed and clapped.

Mr. Larson shut off the TV and pushed the cart aside. He pulled down a rolled up map of the world and tapped the black tip of a pointer onto different countries as he spoke. Mr. Larson said, "If that comedian lived in *this* country or *this* country or *this* country, and if he had told that joke about the president last night, today he would probably be in jail." Pausing dramatically, he moved the pointer to another country. "And if that comedian lived in *this* country and told that joke last night about the president, today he would probably be dead."

Moving the pointer to the United States, Mr. Larson said, "But, of course, that comedian lives in this country, and today he's not in jail, and he's not dead. He's probably sitting somewhere drinking mineral water and thinking of something else to make people laugh again tonight."

Mr. Larson rolled up the map and walked to the side of the classroom. Picking his way among stacks of magazines and a couple of book racks, he stood next to a bulletin board. The board was incredibly cluttered, but in the center there was a small poster printed in faded blue ink that had never had anything stapled over it. At the top it said:

The Bill of Rights
The Ten Original Amendments
to the Constitution of the United States of America

Mr. Larson put the pointer on the word *Constitution* and said, "Now I know we haven't studied the Constitution yet this year, so I'm going to get to the main point here as quickly as I can. The Constitution is like a list of rules, okay? It's a list of rules that tells how our country's government has to be set up. When the Constitution was first written down, some people said it gave too much power to the government and not enough protection to ordinary people. And these people said that before they would agree to the rules of the Constitution, there had to be a bill of rights, a *list* of rights that the government could never take away from people. They didn't want the government to start acting like a cruel king—they had already had one of those, and one was enough."

Mr. Larson tapped on the word *Amendments*. He said, "So they made some *amendments*. This word just means "changes." The Bill of Rights is contained in these ten *changes* that are now a permanent part of the Constitution.

"Now, this is the main idea I want you to get here. They made these ten original amendments even before anyone would agree to the Constitution itself. And the *First* Amendment is first for a reason. It promises that the government cannot get involved in religion—either for or against it. It promises that people are free to express their opinions and ideas—like that comedian last night. And it also says that there is freedom of the press, that the government cannot decide what a news-paper is *allowed* or *not allowed* to print."

Ed caught on right away and his hand shot up. "Does that mean we can print anything we want to in *The Landry News*?" he asked.

Mr. Larson said, "Good question, Ed. What do you think about that, Cara? Can you print anything you want to in *The Landry News*?"

Cara hesitated. "I . . . I'm not sure. I mean, I used to put anything I wanted into the paper because I made the whole thing from beginning to end. But now, I . . . I guess if someone didn't like what we wrote, they could keep us from using the printer, or the computer."

Then Joey said, "But if I used my own computer at home, and I bought my own paper and everything, like, then I could print whatever I felt like, right?"

Sharon's dad was a lawyer. She said, "Yeah, but if you printed a lie about me, my dad would sue you— and then your computer would be *my* computer!"

Mr. Larson said, "You've all raised some good points here. The fact is, when you publish a newspaper, you *do* have to tell the truth. If you get caught lying, someone is likely to sue you—take you to court—like Sharon said. And if a newspaper company publishes the newspaper, then the *owner* of the newspaper gets to decide what may or may not be in the paper."

It was quiet for a moment. Then Ed asked the question that was forming in everyone's mind. "So who is the owner of *The Landry News*? Cara, right?"

Cara shook her head. "Not really—not anymore. And I feel kind of funny having that still be the name of it. I think maybe we should change it to something different."

Joey said, "I don't. You started it, and you're still the

editor in chief, so I vote that we keep the name the same."

Cara blushed at Joey's little speech and blushed even more when the whole class clapped and cheered, agreeing with him.

Mr. Larson brought things back to order. "So that's settled . . . now back to Ed's question about who owns the newspaper . . . LeeAnn?"

LeeAnn said, "Well, the school owns *The Landry News*, right? I mean, like . . . the school buys the paper and the computer and all, so it's the school's, right?"

Mr. Larson smiled. "You could say the owner is the school, and that the head of the school is the principal. But the principal is hired by the school board, and the school board is elected by your parents and the other people in Carlton, and they are the ones who pay the tax money that pays the principal and the teachers, and buys all the paper and the computers and the printers, right?" After a long pause, Mr. Larson said, "There's a lot to think about when you're running a newspaper, isn't there?" And with that the lesson about the Constitution and the Bill of Rights and the freedom of the press was over.

Using the pointer like a gentleman's walking cane, Mr. Larson picked his way through the clutter back to his desk.

It was quiet for another moment or two, and Cara sat there, staring at the Bill of Rights on the bulletin board. She was wondering how much freedom of the press *The Landry News* really had.

A little suspicion formed in the back of her mind that, sooner or later, she'd find out.

CHAPTER 15

REF MAKES TOUGH CALL

ON THE FIRST Friday in December the ninth edition of *The Landry News* was distributed—over three hundred and seventy copies.

Sitting at his desk, Dr. Barnes read his copy carefully. And when he turned to page three, Dr. Barnes finally saw what he had been hoping for, week after week. Smack in the center of the page was the article of his dreams, an article that should not have been printed in a school newspaper. And Dr. Barnes was sure that a majority of the school board would agree with him.

A slow smile spread over his face, and in his mind, Dr. Barnes began planning Mr. Larson's retirement party.

Cara Landry was having the time of her life. *The Landry News* was growing and changing, and she was keeping up with it. By the fourth edition, Joey had to print on both sides of the sheet; and from the fifth edition on, *The Landry News* had needed a second sheet of paper—for section B.

Cara had to plan each edition. She had to read every story and every feature, plus she would help kids with their rewriting and revising. And on Thursdays, when Joey was assembling everything on the computer screen, Cara often had to cut articles or features that took up too much space.

Cara also had to reject whatever she didn't think would be right for *The Landry News*. Chrissy wanted to start a gossip column called "Hot Stuff" about school romances—crushes, rumors, and who was going to be dumped. When Cara asked if the information in her column would always be true, Chrissy had to agree that private notes passed among friends was the best place for this kind of news. And when Josh wanted to start a weekly ranking of the best fifth-grade athletes, Cara told him the list would have to include girls as well as boys. Josh decided to write a piece about ocean kayaking instead.

With all she had to do for the newspaper—not to mention her other schoolwork—Cara was barely able to find time each week to write her own editorial. The editorial was always the last item in the paper, and by the fifth edition that meant it went on page four.

The front page of *The Landry News* was the general news and information page—the main news stories, a summary of school and town events, and a weekly "Homework Countdown" that listed upcoming fifth-grade tests and project due dates. There was always a photograph, and if there was room, the front page also included the weekend weather prediction from the United States Weather Service, complete with little drawings that Alan made of sunshine, clouds, droplets, or snowflakes.

The second page was different advice and information columns that kids kept coming up with, like this question-and-answer column about pets.

Pets? You Bet!
by Carrie Sumner

Dear PYB:

I have a cockatiel bird named Dingo, and all he will say is "pretty bird, pretty bird, pretty bird," over and over again. I talk to him for an hour every day, and I have tried to teach him to say other words, but he isn't interested. No matter what I say to him, and no matter how many times I say it, all he says is "pretty bird, pretty bird, pretty bird." It's driving me nuts. Any advice?

From Crazy in Birdland

Dear Crazy:

I think your bird is mad at you because you named him after an ugly Australian wild dog. He wants to make sure that you know he's a bird, and a pretty one, too. Try changing his name to Wing-Ding or SuperBird or Flier, and see if that works. And if it doesn't, maybe you should think about exactly why you want to be talking to a bird in the first place.

With deep concern, PYB

Alan Rogers had started a column where he interviewed kids about their favorite foods and how they got their parents to buy them.

Snack Attack!

Dedicated to life, liberty, and the pursuit of junk food

by Alan Rogers

AR: So, JJ, [not his real name] I hear you've perfected a way to get your mom to buy sugary cereal and Pop Tarts every time she goes to the store, even if you're not there to beg for them. Sounds too good to be true. Can you tell us about it?

JJ: Believe me, it's true. But it didn't happen overnight. These things take time and planning.

AR: What was the first step?

JJ: I asked my health teacher what meal is the most important one of the day.

AR: But didn't you already know the answer?

JJ: Of course. I knew she would say "Breakfast." And once she did, I went home that afternoon and told my mom that my health teacher said the most important meal of the day is breakfast.

AR: Ahhh! You were laying the foundation, right?

JJ: Exactly. Then I skipped breakfast for the next three days. Mom tried to get me to eat, but I just said, "I don't like anything we have in the house."

AR: Didn't you starve those mornings?

JJ: I had asked my friend ZZ [not his real name] to bring some toast to the bus stop for me, so I was okay. At the end of three days, I mentioned to my mom that I thought I might like some of those Cocoa Puffs, and that the chocolate and marshmallow Pop Tarts might be something I could eat, too. The next morning, there they were, like magic—right on the kitchen counter.

AR: Well, JJ, that's certainly an inspiring story, and I know our readers will appreciate your sharing it with us all.

There was a book review every week, a video-game tips column, a "Best of the Web" listing, and a "Best TV Movies of the Weekend" column. Since Christmas and Hanukkah were not that far off, there was a "Holiday Countdown"—a column listing the top ten presents that kids on the red and blue teams were hoping for.

Tommy read a lot, and when he was in fourth grade he had started collecting slang expressions that he thought were funny. He eventually discovered that there were whole dictionaries of slang. He asked Cara if he could have a column about slang, and the editor in chief said okay, as long as everything in the column had a G rating. Tommy agreed, and a column called "That Slang Thang" was born.

Section B—the second sheet of *The Landry News*—was a hodgepodge. If there were some good columns that wouldn't fit on page two, they ended up in section B. There were two regular weekly comic strips and usually a cartoon or two, as well as short stories and vacation travel stories about places kids had visited—like the Grand Canyon or the Field Museum. There were poems and jokes, and LeeAnn had surprised everybody with a completely creepy mystery story that had a new installment every week.

And then, on the Wednesday before Thanksgiving, Michael Morton came up to Cara after school at her locker and asked if he could give her a story that a friend of his wanted to have printed in the newspaper. Michael was a computer whiz, the kid who did the "Best of the Web" listing for the paper each week. He kept mostly to himself. Cara said, "Sure, Michael. I'll be glad to look at it." Cara stuck the sheets of paper in her backpack, grabbed her coat, and ran to catch her bus.

Late that night, Cara remembered the story, got it out of her book bag, and lay across her bed to read it. It was only two pages, written in black ballpoint. There were tons of cross outs and smears on each page, and the writer had pushed down so hard with his pen that the back side of each sheet reminded Cara of Braille, the raised alphabet

Michael Morton, computer whiz and loner.

for blind people.

There was no name at the beginning, just the title "Lost and Found." The story began with this sentence: "When I heard that my parents were getting divorced, the first thing I did was run to my room, grab my baseball bat, and pound all my Little League trophies into bits."

Cara was hooked. The person in the story was a boy, and Cara was amazed at how similar his feelings were to the ones she'd had when her dad left. The same kind of anger, the same kind of blind lashing out. And finally, there was the same sort of calming down, facing facts. The story did not end very hopefully, but the boy saw that life would still go on, and that both his dad and his mom still loved him just as much, maybe more.

When Cara finished reading, she was choked up and her eyes were wet. She noticed that there was no name at the end of the story either. That's when it hit her that this was not fiction. It was real life. It was Michael Morton's own story.

Cara slid off her bed and went out to the living room, drying her eyes on the sleeve of her robe. Her mom was on the couch, watching the end of a show, so Cara sat with her for about five minutes.

When the show ended, Cara picked up the channel changer and shut off the TV. Then she handed her mom the story. "Would you read this for me, Mom? Someone wants me to put it in the next edition of the newspaper."

Joanna Landry took off her glasses and said, "Why sure, honey, I'd love to."

Cara watched her mom's face as she read, and she saw her mom's eyes fill up with tears when she got to the end.

Blinking back her tears, her mother turned toward Cara on the couch and said, "If I didn't know better, I'd have thought you wrote this sad little story yourself, Cara honey. I think it's *awfully* good, don't you?" Cara had brought a copy of each edition of *The Landry News* home, and Mrs. Landry had proudly taped them all onto the wall in the kitchen. She was thrilled to see Cara doing something so good—and good-hearted—enjoying herself and using her talents. Handing back the smudged pages, her mother asked, "So are you going to put it in the paper?"

Cara said, "I'm not sure. I think I'd better talk to Mr. Larson about it."

And after the long Thanksgiving weekend, Cara had her mom drop her off at school early so she could show the story to Mr. Larson before school.

Mr. Larson adjusted his reading glasses and took the pages over by the windows where the light was better. Three minutes later, he was finished, and his eyes were shining. "This boy has certainly caught the essence of a hard experience here," he said, reaching for his handkerchief.

Cara nodded and said, "So maybe I shouldn't put it in the newspaper, right?"

Mr. Larson looked down at the story again, then handed it back to Cara. "Tell me what *you* think about it, Cara."

Cara was quiet while Mr. Larson walked over to his desk, sat down, and picked up his coffee cup. "Well, first of all," she said, "I'm just sure this is a true story, so it's like telling the whole school about some family's private business. Someone might not like that—like the mom or the dad, for instance. Divorce is a pretty messy subject, don't you think? I mean, that part about him running away, and the police coming and everything—"

Cara paused, waiting for Mr. Larson's reaction. He took a sip of coffee, looked out the window, and then back to Cara's face. "You said you are sure this is a true story. Is it trying to hurt anyone?"

Cara shook her head and said, "No—in fact, it really helped me," and then she blushed at what she'd said.

Mr. Larson pretended not to notice and quickly said,

"Well, it helped me, too."

"So I should put it in the newspaper, right?" said Cara.

Mr. Larson said, "I appreciate your talking to me about it, but that's a decision that the editor in chief should make. I will say that whatever you decide to do, I will support you completely."

Four days later, the first Friday in December, in the middle of page three of the ninth edition of *The Landry News*, there was a story by an anonymous writer, a story called "Lost and Found."

It was the same story that Dr. Barnes was so excited about.

CHAPTER 16

SALVAGE CREW INSPECTS WRECKAGE

ON THE MONDAY after the ninth edition came out, Mr. Larson got a large brown envelope from Dr. Barnes, hand delivered to him before school by Mrs. Cormier—just in case he forgot to check his mailbox in the office. There were two items in the envelope. The first was a copy of a letter from Dr. Barnes to the school superintendent and each of the seven members of the school board. It requested an emergency meeting concerning "a disciplinary proceeding against Mr. Karl Larson." The letter stated that "Mr. Larson allowed the attached article to be published in a classroom newspaper under his supervision, and over three hundred copies were distributed throughout the school and community." Other phrases in the letter included, "lack of professional judgment," "disregard for individual privacy," "unprofessional behavior," "inappropriate use of school resources," and "insensitivity to community values." A photocopy of the third page of the ninth edition of *The Landry News* was stapled to the letter, with the story about the divorce circled.

The second item in the envelope was a letter to Mr. Larson from Dr. Barnes, informing him of the intended disciplinary action. The letter told Mr. Larson that this would be a public hearing and he might want to have his own lawyer present at the meeting. The secretary of the teachers' union at the school had been informed about the hearing. Dr. Barnes also reminded Mr. Larson that, if he wished, he could choose to resign. If he resigned, there would be no need for a disciplinary proceeding. He could quietly retire, and that would be the end of it. Dr. Barnes ended the letter by saying that publication of *The Landry News* must cease immediately.

Mr. Larson slumped back in his chair, his long arms hanging limp at his sides. He felt as if he'd been kicked in the stomach. The threat of losing his job was certainly real. Ever since Dr. Barnes arrived at Denton seven years ago, Mr. Larson had known that it was only a matter of time before something like this happened. And Mr. Larson thought, "Maybe I deserve this. I've been a rotten teacher, more like half a teacher, for a long time now. Maybe this school will be a lot better off without me. I've probably got this coming."

But Karl Larson was absolutely sure of one thing. The *kids* did not deserve this one little bit. *The Landry News* had become something wonderful. And the thing that hurt him the most was that because of *his* problems—not the kids' problems—Dr. Barnes was going to use this innocent little newspaper as the whip to send him packing.

But sitting there on his chair in his cluttered room, Mr. Larson turned a corner.

He forgot about his own problems. He began to think about how he could protect his students from the ugliness of this situation. He wanted to be sure that not one of them was harmed or upset in any way. As he began to think about the kids, all the heaviness and burden seemed to drop away. Then all at once, Mr. Larson got an idea, and he sat bolt upright in his chair.

And the thought that formed clearly in his mind was incredibly simple. It was a plan that would protect all the kids, and it would protect him, and it might even protect Dr. Barnes as well.

And one word summed up the whole solution: *teach.*

The newest copy of *The Landry News* lay there on his desk next to the letters from Dr. Barnes. Mr. Larson looked from one to the other, and he smiled. Everyone else could get as upset and angry and worried as they wanted to, but he was not going to worry. Why?

Simple. Because his kids were going to see this whole thing as one large, exciting, learning experience about the First Amendment and the freedom of the press.

And who was going to transform this mess into a thing of educational beauty?

Mr. Larson, Teacher.

CHAPTER 17

RESCUE SQUAD TACKLES CLEANUP

CARA FELT AWFUL. Mr. Larson had just told the class that *The Landry News* could not be published anymore—at least, not right away. He had made transparencies of the letters from Dr. Barnes and put them on the overhead projector so the whole class could see them while he explained what was happening. Then he showed a transparency of the story about the boy and the divorce.

Mr. Larson said, "Now, it's important for each of us to think very clearly about all this." Glancing over the twenty-three faces looking up at him from the darkened room, his eyes met Cara's for a moment before looking back at the screen. "Some of you might be tempted to think, 'Oh, if only we had not published this *one* little story, everything would be all right.' But is that true? No, it's not. Because if it wasn't *this* story, it would have been some *other* story or some review of a movie or a review of a book that someone does not like. You have to remember that publishing *this* story was the right thing to do. It's a wonderful story and a brave story, and I know that it was very good for a lot of people to read it and think about it—and a lot of people have told me that it's the *best* thing *The Landry News* has published so far. So that's the first thing—the paper just told the truth."

It *sounded* good—hearing Mr. Larson say it like that—but it didn't make Cara feel any better. She had a copy of the newspaper on her desk, and her thoughts went round and round. *I should have known better—I should have thought about Mr. Larson instead of the stupid newspaper. I should have just handed that story right back to Michael Morton. I should have known better.* The classroom snapped back into focus for Cara as Mr. Larson turned off the overhead projector and Sharon flipped on the lights.

As the kids squinted and blinked, Mr. Larson said, "So someone thinks that divorce is too personal to write about in a school newspaper. I'm the teacher in charge, so I'm the one responsible, so it looks like *I* am suddenly in trouble. But *am* I?"

Picking his way over to the bulletin board, Mr. Larson tapped the Bill of Rights poster and then rested the pointer on the First Amendment. "Am *I* in trouble here, or is something *else* in trouble?"

Mr. Larson could see by their faces that all the kids got the idea. It was Cara who said it. She said, "It's the

First Amendment that's in trouble—the freedom of the press is in trouble." Then she frowned and said, "But I still think *you're* in trouble, too."

Mr. Larson grinned, touched by Cara's concern. "Well, I am perfectly sure that there's nothing for any of us to worry about. We've all been doing good work here, and now, thanks to this situation, we're going to get to learn about the freedom of the press in a way that very few teachers or kids will ever get to. Besides, I've been in trouble before, and let me tell you—I think this is the *best* trouble I've ever been in."

A few of the kids laughed a little when Mr. Larson said that, but not Cara. Walking toward the front of the room, Mr. Larson glanced at her. She sat stiffly in her chair, glaring at her copy of *The Landry News*, biting her lower lip.

Back at his desk, Mr. Larson picked up a stack of stapled handouts and passed them around. "This is your study packet for this unit. Take a look at page one with me."

For the next ten minutes, Mr. Larson walked the class through all the steps in the process—things that would happen before the hearing, at the hearing, and after the hearing. He wanted to make sure there was nothing mysterious, nothing scary about any of it. He did not paint Dr. Barnes as a villain or himself as a victim. It was not us against them. It was just a contest between two different ideas of what was right, what was the greatest good for the greatest number.

As Mr. Larson calmly explained everything, Cara relaxed a little. He wasn't just pretending to be brave—Cara could tell he was truly excited about all of this. And when Mr. Larson squinted and rubbed his hands together and said, "It's like we get to mess around in our own private democracy laboratory!" even Cara had to smile.

She flipped ahead to look at the last page of the handout, looking for a clue about where this whole thing would end up. There was only one word on the last page: *Conclusions*. The rest of the page was blank.

That blank page was actually comforting to Cara. She was used to looking at blank pages, and she was used to filling them up with things that were true and good. To Cara, that final page looked like hope.

CHAPTER 18

CENSORSHIP+ COMPUTERS =NO WAY

JOEY SAT NEXT TO CARA on the bus that Monday afternoon. He was quiet, and so was Cara. Even after all the explanations, she still felt responsible for the whole mess, especially for what was happening to Mr. Larson. There was a lot to think about.

Joey broke the silence with a question. "So you're going to keep on publishing the paper anyway, right?"

Cara's ponytail wagged as she shook her head. "We can't, Joey. If we don't obey the rules, it will just make it harder for Mr. Larson."

They were quiet again, looking out the windows on opposite sides of the bus for the next two stops. Then as if a puppet master had rotated their heads at exactly the same moment, they faced each other and both started talking at once. "But the letter said *The Landry News*!" said Cara. "It didn't say stop making *all* newspapers!"

"I know, I know!" blurted Joey. "As long as we don't make a newspaper at school or pass it out there, we can publish anything we want to—as long as it's true!" Joey was practically shouting. "And why? Because it's a free country, that's why!"

Cara had hold of Joey's arm, squeezing it, and her voice had gone up an octave. "So you've got a computer, right?" she asked. Joey nodded, and Cara went on. "And you've got a printer, too?"

Joey nodded again and said, "It's not as big as the one at school, but it's a good one, and it even prints in color! We'll have to redesign everything for a smaller sheet size, but that's okay, because it's a whole new paper anyway!"

Cara stayed on the bus and rode to Joey's stop. LeeAnn and Alan and Ed had joined the conversation, and in four minutes they had already taken a unanimous vote on the new name that Ed came up with. By the time they got off the bus and had begun to walk the last block to Joey's house, the publishing committee had offered Cara Landry the job of editor in chief for a brand new newspaper, the *Guardian*. And she accepted, provided that the motto of the new paper could still be the same: Truth and Mercy.

Halfway through science class on Friday morning, Mrs. Cormier arrived with an invitation for Cara Landry. The principal wanted to talk to her.

A few minutes later, Cara sat across the desk from Dr. Barnes. She was glad she had experience in these matters. Cara had observed quite a few angry school administrators—at least one a week for most of fourth grade. She had developed what she called the Mad-O-Meter. It was a scale from one to ten, where one equals "mild tremor" and ten equals "erupting volcano." Judging from the color of his face, the rate of his breathing, the flare of his nostrils, and the fact that both doors of his office were closed, Cara thought that Dr. Barnes was probably at about eight—the "steaming mud slide" stage. She waited politely for Dr. Barnes to begin the conversation.

He slid a copy of the *Guardian* across the desk and turned it around so she could see it. The headline of the lead story was WHY THE FIRST AMENDMENT IS FIRST. The article laid out the situation involving *The Landry News*, Mr. Larson, Denton Elementary School, and the Carlton school board. Dr. Barnes had to admit to himself that it was a masterful piece of reporting. The story was honest, it was impartial, and it lived up to the newspaper's motto.

Dr. Barnes cleared his throat and said, "What is your connection with this newspaper, Cara?"

Cara disliked being treated like a baby. The masthead of the newspaper was on the front page, as plain as the nose on Dr. Barnes's face—and his nose was very plain from where Cara was sitting. The masthead listed all the workers on the paper. All twenty-three kids in Mr. Larson's afternoon class had wanted their names in the masthead, and each had done something to help get the *Guardian* pulled together in record time. Cara and Joey had gotten the idea on Monday afternoon, and the first edition had been ready to distribute today, Friday morning.

Dr. Barnes was a tempting target, but Cara didn't get snippy, and she didn't get angry. She didn't even get sarcastic. She pointed meekly at the masthead. "It says what everyone does for the paper right here in the masthead. I'm the editor in chief."

Dr. Barnes said, "I see. And weren't you the editor in chief of *The Landry News* as well?"

Cara nodded. "Yes, until Mr. Larson told us we had to stop publishing it for a while."

Cara already knew exactly where Dr. Barnes was headed with this. She did not want to suffer through a long and boring cat-and-mouse question session. Cara wanted to lay it all out on the table. And she also wanted Dr. Barnes to know right away that she saw what he was up to.

So before Dr. Barnes could ask his next question, Cara said, "You probably think that this paper is just *The Landry News*, only with a different name. But it's not, Dr. Barnes. First, *The Landry News* was written and assembled and produced during school hours on school property, using school equipment and supplies. The *Guardian* was written outside of school, and it was produced in a private home using privately owned equipment and supplies.

"Second, *The Landry News* was distributed to students by other students during school hours on school property. The *Guardian* is distributed by a group of kids to their friends on privately owned property before or after school hours.

"And third, *The Landry News* was supervised by Mr. Larson, and from the second edition to the ninth and final edition, Mr. Larson saw every copy of it. The *Guardian* was thought up and created independently by only the friends listed here in the masthead, without adults being involved at all."

Cara hadn't meant to push Dr. Barnes up toward the "erupting volcano" point, but the lava was starting to flow anyway. He glared at her and jabbed at the paper with his blunt index finger. "Young lady, do you mean to tell me that you did not intend to distribute these papers at school today? These papers are all over this school and all over the floors in all the buses."

Cara said mildly, "We didn't bring a single paper to school, honest. We have friends at almost every bus stop, and we had our newspapers ready this morning, so we handed them out. We even made sure that we stayed in someone's yard instead of on the sidewalk—because the sidewalk is owned by the town, and when kids are waiting for the school bus there, it's like school property. But after we handed the papers to our friends, where they took them—well, that wasn't up to us."

Cara leaned forward and pointed at the little symbol Joey had added to the bottom of the front page. "We even reminded kids to be sure to recycle the paper."

Cara sat up straighter in her chair and said, "Hey—I know! Next week, we'll add 'Please don't litter,' and see if that helps." Cara paused a minute, smiling absently at Dr. Barnes. Even his ear lobes were red now.

"And guess what?" said Cara brightly.

"What?" said Dr. Barnes, almost in a whisper.

"If you flip that paper over, down at the bottom you can see our Internet address—isn't that cool? By this time next week the *Guardian* will be online, and our Internet edition won't use any paper at all! No litter! Isn't that great?!"

Dr. Barnes disliked displays of emotion, especially anger. It wasn't professional. So in an abnormally quiet voice, Dr. Barnes said, "Yes, that's a fine idea, Cara. Well then. Please . . . go out to the front office now . . . and ask Mrs. Cormier . . . for a pass . . . to your class. And close the door behind you . . . please."

Two minutes later Cara left the office. Dr. Barnes's door was still shut.

If it hadn't been against the rules, Cara Landry would have skipped down the hall, all the way back to her science class.

CHAPTER 19

DECEMBER TO BE WARMER THAN NORMAL

MR. LARSON HAD not been a favorite among his fellow teachers in recent years. He was too standoffish, too solitary. Most of the other teachers disapproved of the wildness of his classes. To the teachers who had been around a long time, seeing Mr. Larson become less and less professional about his teaching had been especially sad, because they remembered the old Karl Larson.

But *The Landry News* had gotten everyone's attention. Every teacher had watched the newspaper grow from one sheet to two, then to three and four. They saw the quality of the writing and marveled at it. "Fifth-graders!" they said to each other as they passed the *News* around the teachers' room. "Larson's got *fifth*-graders doing this kind of work! Amazing!"

Most of the teachers had met Cara Landry. They knew that the success of the newspaper was due in large part to her hard work and energy. But they also knew that it was no accident that *The Landry News* had come out of room 145. Without the experience and the guidance and the understanding of Karl Larson, *The Landry News* could not have become what it was.

So, when the teachers' union representative was notified about the disciplinary hearing, the faculty rallied around Mr. Larson. There was a teacher's meeting, and the vote of support was unanimous.

Right away, Ms. Steinert wrote up a press release about the situation. A committee duplicated the eight copies of *The Landry News* and sent sets of them along with the information sheet to every newspaper, radio, and TV station in the greater Chicago area. They printed up handbills with the divorce story on it and mailed it to the home of every taxpayer in Carlton, asking the question, "Should someone be fired because of this?"

Mr. Larson's wife was active in the Chicago teachers' union, and each elementary, junior high, and high school in the metropolitan area received a copy of the press release about the hearing and the charges. The president of the union had made a statement on WGN about the case and the importance of supporting free speech and academic freedom.

Of course, all the parents of the kids in Mr. Larson's class already knew about *The Landry News*. Many of them had been making their own photocopies of the paper for grandparents and aunts and uncles, so everyone could see the wonderful things those bright kids in Mr. Larson's class were writing and thinking and learning.

A reporter from the *Chicago Tribune* followed up and learned that the kids were now publishing a different paper, the *Guardian*, on their own, including an Internet edition. Four days later, the online *Guardian* had a free link from the *Tribune*'s own homepage—and three days after that, the *Sun Times* followed suit.

Before the superintendent had even posted a notice on the town's cable TV channel to list the time and place of the hearing, there had already been articles about the situation in both of the big Chicago newspapers. Mr. Larson had even been interviewed in the Sunday *Tribune*, and a reporter from Channel Nine's evening news had come to the apartments at Edgewater Village to interview Cara Landry.

Cara hadn't liked the interview or the reporter, a woman with bright orange hair. It was a cold and windy afternoon, but the reporter wanted to talk outdoors. She said she looked better on camera in natural light. Barking orders, she got the camera crew and the sound guy in position next to some evergreen bushes.

After finding the best angle for the shot, she faced the camera, smiled, and said, "I'm Jordy Matlin, coming to you live from the Edgewater Apartments in Carlton. This is the home of Cara Landry, a young lady whose newspaper is at the center of a local controversy. Now Cara, tell our viewers, was it your teacher or your principal who got you in trouble about this newspaper?"

Cara wasn't expecting such a question. She froze up.

The reporter stopped smiling, lowered her microphone, and yelled, "Cut!" Bending so close that Cara could smell the acrid scent of her hair spray, Jordy Matlin said, "This is the part where I ask you questions, and you answer them, okay? All you have to do is listen to the question, and when I hold out the microphone, you talk. All right?" The camerawoman cued the reporter with a count of five, and then Jordy asked Cara the same question. "Now, Cara, tell us, was it your teacher or your principal who got you in trouble about this newspaper?" This time, Cara was ready. She had remembered that this was just like writing for the newspaper, only she'd be talking instead. All she had to do was tell the truth in a kind way. So Cara said, "Neither. And I'm not in trouble. The newspaper's not even in trouble, really. It's just a difference of opinion about what should go into a newspaper made at a school."

The reporter tilted the microphone back toward herself and said, "This story about a divorce that you published—didn't you think this would cause some problems? If this isn't just a story, say, if this really happened, then some family's business has been spread all

Jordy Matlin, reporter for WQRR in Chicago.

over town. And, of course, many churchgoers think divorce itself is bad. Didn't you think there might be a problem here?"

Cara looked into the camera and said, "I wasn't thinking about anything except giving someone the chance to tell a story—and it's a story that I think has been good for a lot of kids to read."

The camera stayed on Cara's face for another three seconds, and then the reporter said, "Cut," quickly shook Cara's hand, and turned on her heel and clicked off across the parking lot, talking with her producer. Cara heard her say, "Now we need a shot of the school, and fifteen seconds each with the principal, the superintendent, and the school board president. And we've got to find this teacher that they're trying to ax. We can lay out some copies of the kid's newspapers and get a collage shot back in the studio before we do the full mix. Ted tells me he's holding two minutes for us in the local segment, but we have to really hustle if we're going to make it." All the newspeople piled into two white vans and roared off toward the center of town.

Cara was disappointed. She thought there would be more to it than that. She'd only gotten to say about three sentences, and it was such a complicated story. Fifty or sixty words wasn't enough. And what had the reporter called Mr. Larson . . . "this teacher they're trying to ax"? Cara winced at that, wishing she had used her moment on camera to say something that would have helped take the heat off Mr. Larson.

Joanna Landry came over and put Cara's coat around her shoulders. Cara smiled up at her mom and said, "Now I know why I like newspaper stories better than TV news stories." Her mom nodded and smiled. "That reporter was kind of a tough bird. Still, you did just fine, Cara honey. Now let's get in out of this wind."

Based on the number of phone calls received at the superintendent's office, the location of the hearing was moved from the town hall to the high school auditorium so there would be enough room for everyone who was planning to attend.

During the ten days before the hearing, Mr. Larson and his afternoon class kept track of each development and how it related to the First Amendment. The kids saw the impact of the newspaper and television coverage. They studied Mr. Larson's interview in the newspaper and compared it to Cara's TV interview, and then compared them to other interviews of Dr.

Barnes and the superintendent. They split into teams and had debates, and they put a whole new layer of clippings and cartoons and news photos onto Mr. Larson's bulletin boards.

Mr. Larson was happier than he had been for many years. By the time the day of the hearing arrived, he was ready to walk in with his head held high. All of his students were planning to be there.

For most people, this was simply a disciplinary hearing. But for Mr. Larson and his students, it was the last lesson in a unit about the most interesting subject they had ever studied.

CHAPTER 20

HOME TEAM GOES FOR BROKE

SHORTLY BEFORE 7:30 on a Tuesday night in December, Mr. Larson straightened his necktie, kissed his wife, then turned to walk down the sloped aisle of the high school auditorium. A row of folding tables had been set up in front of the auditorium stage. After he sat down across from Dr. Barnes at the first table, Mr. Larson turned his head and looked out into the audience. It looked to him like there were at least four hundred people in the room.

His wife had settled near the back and was smiling at him, all warmth and support. The kids from his class were scattered all over the place, sitting with one or both of their parents. Cara and her mother were in the fourth row, and when he looked at them, Cara gave him a nervous smile and waved shyly. Mr. Larson felt self-conscious up there at the front of the hall, but he did not feel alone.

There was something that Mr. Larson had not discussed with the kids in his class. It was entirely possible that the freedom of the press would win *its* battle, and that *he* would still lose his job.

True, public opinion mattered. Newspaper reporters and camera crews from two of the three major TV stations were here. But at the end of the night, it would all depend on how the school board voted. Mr. Larson knew that out of the seven members, three would love to see him leave, and two others were not very fond of him. It was going to be an uphill battle.

At exactly seven-thirty, the superintendent called the meeting to order. The school board president, Mrs. Deopolis, read the call-to-meeting notice and then introduced Dr. Barnes. Since it was Dr. Barnes who had brought the complaint, he was required to speak first.

"Madam President," he began, "on Friday, December seventh, I read the newest edition of this student newspaper and found a story about divorce that I did not think was appropriate. As you know, I immediately brought the article to the attention of the board and the superintendent. You apparently agreed that the content was not appropriate, and since Mr. Larson had accepted responsibility for the content of the newspaper, you agreed that this disciplinary hearing was needed. Madam President, will you please explain to those present what the board found to be inappropriate in the story?"

As Dr. Barnes sat down, Mrs. Deopolis leaned closer to her microphone and said, "Yes, Dr. Barnes. We found that the subject matter and the description of the boy's suffering was too personal, and that the topic of divorce is too mature a theme to be treated in this way in an elementary school newspaper. The board feels that by allowing this to be published, Mr. Larson made a very serious error in judgment. In light of past complaints about Mr. Larson's abilities and practices as a classroom teacher, we agreed that this hearing was necessary." Turning to Mr. Larson, Mrs. Deopolis asked, "Mr. Larson, do you have a lawyer present or will you be speaking for yourself?"

Mr. Larson stood up stiffly, talking into a hand-held microphone. "I will be speaking for myself, Madam President." Stepping away from the table, Mr. Larson addressed the board members. "I see this issue of the story in *The Landry News* in very simple terms. Yes, Dr. Barnes made me responsible for the content of the paper, and I passed that responsibility on to the students. It is true that Dr. Barnes asked to see each copy of the newspaper before it was printed, and I refused that request. But Dr. Barnes did not *insist* on previewing each paper, which, as principal, he could have. Instead, he left the responsibility with me. He gave me no guidelines about what topics were not appropriate, nor does the school board have any clear policies regarding school newspapers. According to the *Hazelwood* Supreme Court decision, a school board must have a clear set of policies in force in order to censor a student newspaper."

Mr. Larson paused and looked around at Dr. Barnes. "So, as I see it, I am being accused of allowing something to happen that no one ever informed me I should not have allowed to happen in the first place. Either that, or the real issue here is those past complaints about my teaching practices that Madam President has mentioned."

Mr. Larson walked back to his place, opened his briefcase, and pulled out a copy of the article. "As part of my statement, I would like to read out loud the entire story from the newspaper so that all present and also all those watching at home on the town cable TV channel can judge for themselves its appropriateness or inappropriateness." The board members began hurriedly whispering among themselves, their hands cupped over their microphones.

The whispering stopped, and Mrs. Deopolis said, "Since it is a part of your defense, you have the right to read the story into the record, Mr. Larson."

A woman in the sixth row immediately stood up and raised her hand. Mrs. Deopolis nodded to her, and a Boy Scout trotted over to her with another portable microphone. "Thank you, Madam President. My name is Allie Morton, and my son Michael has asked if he may read the story aloud. He's the boy who wrote it, and it's about the divorce our family went through last year."

Almost everyone in the auditorium seemed to gasp at once. But Cara Landry didn't gasp. She had known this was coming. She had called Michael a week ago to ask him to read his story at the meeting. She told him it would help Mr. Larson if people could see that this was a true story. At first Michael said no. He thought he would be too scared. But after he talked it over with his mom, he called Cara back and said he would do it—for Mr. Larson. Cara sat up on the edge of her seat to see what would happen.

After another hurried conference among the board, it was agreed that Michael Morton could read his own words aloud for the record. He squeezed his way past knees and seat backs in the sixth row and walked down the aisle to where Mr. Larson stood. Mr. Larson handed Michael the story and held the microphone for him. Michael brushed the mop of brown hair out of his eyes, looked once at his mom in the sixth row, and then at Cara Landry in the fourth row. He focused on the page, gulped, and began to read, squinting because of the bright lights held up by the TV camera crews.

Lost and Found

When I heard that my parents were getting divorced, the first thing I did was run to my room, grab my baseball bat, and pound all my Little League trophies into bits.

I felt like I wanted to run away. I have a lot of friends who have divorced parents, but I never thought it would happen in my family. I felt like I was lost. This was going to ruin everything.

My mom told me that my dad was going to move out and live somewhere else. She kept saying things like "Don't worry" and "Everything will be all right" and "Things like this just happen." And she said that I would still get to see my dad and that I could talk to him whenever I wanted to. I didn't believe her.

My dad took me out to a restaurant. He wanted to talk to me. He said I wouldn't understand, but that he just didn't love my mom anymore. He was right—that was the part I couldn't understand. I mean, sometimes I yell "I hate you!" at my mom and my dad, and some days I feel like I hate everybody. But I don't really, and pretty soon everything's okay again. I know I could never stop loving my dad. And I could never stop loving Mom, either. So I couldn't see how my dad could stop loving her. And I thought that if my dad could stop loving Mom, then he could probably stop loving me, too.

When Dad went to pay for the food, I ran out of the restaurant and hid in the bushes by the parking lot. I saw him come outside and look for me, and he was yelling my name and he was really scared and worried. And I was glad. I watched until my dad got in the car and used his telephone, and then he drove off toward our house, really fast.

I walked over to my friend Josh's house, but

he wasn't home. Then I just walked and walked. It was way after dark when I got home. There was a police car in front of my house. When I walked in, my mom ran over to hug me, but I wouldn't let her. My dad said I was in big trouble, and that I was grounded. But I just said, "How are you going to ground me? You're not even going to be here to see *anything* I do." Then I went to my room and slammed the door as hard as I could.

That was about a year ago. My dad did move out, and now he's already married again. I never did really run away, not even for an afternoon. But I used to cry a lot, late at night. I know some kids will think that's a sissy thing, but I couldn't help it. And one day my mom was late getting home from work, and there wasn't a message, and there was no answer at her office, and I got so scared, and I ran to her room to look in her closet to see if her dresses were still there. It was stupid, but I was afraid that maybe she had moved out, too.

Sometimes I'm not as happy as I used to be, but I try not to show it. I think my mom is happier now, but if I get unhappy, it ruins things for her and then it's hard for both of us.

Things aren't so bad now, just different. I found out that my mom told the truth back at the beginning, because everything is mostly all right, and when she said "things like this just happen," that was right too. Now I know that something like this can just happen, because it happened to me.

And I also found out that my dad still loves me. And I even know that he still loves Mom, only not in a married way. It's not that I see him a lot or anything, because I don't. He's not with me every day, or at bedtimes, except one weekend a month. But I know he still loves me. I just know it, and sometimes just knowing something has to be enough.

Michael Morton, author of "Lost and Found," reads in defense of his teacher, Mr. Larson.

When Michael finished reading, people all around the auditorium were fishing around for tissues and handkerchiefs. There was a spontaneous burst of applause, and he made his way back to his seat. After Michael sat down, his mom put her arm around his shoulders and squeezed.

When it was quiet again, Mr. Larson said, "Thank you, Michael." Then he held up the story Michael had just read and said, "How could someone say that *this* is not appropriate content for elementary school children to read and think about? Parents and others who have very good motives—people like Dr. Barnes and all of us who want only the best for children—we may not like to admit that things like divorce create very real problems for children, but they do. And if children are honest enough to admit that, why can't we?

"My teaching style is unconventional, and Dr. Barnes and I have disagreed about that since he arrived here seven years ago. Could I have been a better teacher during that time? Yes. I admit that. But what has happened with this newspaper—and that includes allowing this story to be published—is some of the best work I have done in all my nineteen years as a teacher. If I am to be fired, please, let it be for something other than this."

Everyone, even Dr. Barnes, knows that in an auditorium with four hundred people on their feet and cheering, with the TV cameras rolling, and the reporters scribbling in their notebooks, it's not a good idea to fire the person the crowd is applauding.

In less than a minute, while the audience was still clapping and cheering, Mrs. Deopolis took a quick poll of the school board and announced for the record that the disciplinary action against Mr. Karl Larson, Teacher, was dismissed.

Cara Landry had done as Mr. Larson asked and stopped publishing *The Landry News*. But even though the *Guardian* had kept her busy, Cara had not stopped *writing The Landry News*, and she had not stopped printing it. As the crowd began to leave, Cara stayed in her seat in the fourth row and turned to watch.

Joey and Ed stood at doors on the north side of the auditorium; LeeAnn and Sharon took the two doors at the south side. They were handing out a special edition of *The Landry News*.

Cara reached into her coat, pulled out a copy, and carried it down to Mr. Larson, who was surrounded by reporters. He stopped midsentence when Cara put it into his hand, and looked from the paper to Cara's face and then back to the paper. Cara stood to one side and watched quietly as he read the whole thing.

The special edition was only the front side of one page. It had a single headline—**LARSON IS VINDICATED!**

And the only other thing on the page was an editorial.

From the Editor's Desk
The Heart of the News

When *The Landry News* chose the motto "Truth and Mercy," we did it to remind ourselves that a good newspaper must have both. A newspaper that is only filled with cold, hard facts is like an iceberg, crushing anything that gets in its way. A newspaper that only looks at the soft and gentle side of things is like a jellyfish, floppy and spineless. From the start, *The Landry News* has tried to be a balanced, good-hearted newspaper.

I have been going to school now for six years. Some of those school years were soft and gentle, and some were hard, cold years. It depended a lot on what kind of teachers I had. It also depended on me.

The best year so far is this year. This year has a good heart. And that's because the heart of this year is Mr. Larson.

The kids who work on the *News* noticed that about fifteen years ago Mr. Larson was chosen Best Teacher of the Year three years in a row. We are sure that sometime soon Mr. Larson will be Teacher of the Year again. For all of us who work on *The Landry News*, he already is.

And that's the view this week from the *News* desk.

Cara Landry, Editor in Chief

The heart of this year is Mr. Larson.

ANDREW CLEMENTS remembers: "As a teacher, I knew many students like Cara, girls and boys who are more engaged than they look, who may have suffered, who feel deeply about things, who have a lot to say, but often spend their whole school careers unnoticed. I also knew teachers like Mr. Larson—men and women who have had to work their way through hard times professionally and personally, and yet have managed to keep on loving, to continue giving. . . . This book is about how we earn our second chances."

Andrew Clements is the author of over forty books for children, including *Frindle, The Report Card,* and most recently, *Lunch Money*. He lives with his family outside Boston, Massachusetts.